# Cooking Around the Country with Kids:

## USA Regional Recipes
### and
### Fun Activities

**Amy Houts**

Snaptail Press
Division of Images Unlimited
Maryville, Missouri

All inquiries should be addressed to:
Snaptail Press
Division of Images Unlimited Publishing
P.O. Box 305
Maryville, MO  64468
660-582-4605

info@imagesunlimitedpub.com     http://wwwsnaptail.com

Interior Layout Design and Front Cover:
MK Bassett-Harvey/Harding House Publishing Service, Inc.


**Library of Congress Cataloging-in-Publication Data**

Houts, Amy, 1957
 Cooking around the country with kids:USA regional recipes and fun activities / by Amy Houts.
    p. cm.
Includes index.
ISBN 978-0-930643-20-1
1. Cookery, American—Juvenile literature. 2. Food habits—United States—History. I. Title.
TX715.H3833 2009
641.5973—dc22
2009016257

**ATTN: Quantity discounts are available to your Educational Institution, Organization, Corporation, or Industry** for reselling, educational purposes, subscription incentives, gifts or fund raising campaigns.

For more information, please contact the publisher at
Images Unlimited Publishing, 124 N. Grand Ave., Maryville, MO  64468
800-366-1695 —lee@imagesunlimitedpub.com

First Edition
10 9 8 7 6 5 4 3 2 1


Printed in the United States of America

# Acknowledgements

I want to thank my husband, Steve Houts, and daughters, Emily and Sarah Dettmer, my parents, Arthur and Betty Farber, my publisher, Lee Jackson, as well as each person who contributed to this book: Laura Houts, Kay Walsh, Cindy Brown, Jan White, Margaret Preus, Ericka Kinsey, Shelly Robertson, Mary Fran Stransky, Marjean Ehlers, Marla Burnsides, Cindy Chapman, Diane Sudhoff, Lisa Dalton, Carol McAdams, Winifred Laber, Shari Barr, and others. I appreciate all your help and couldn't have completed this cookbook without your loving support.

My love and deep appreciation to all,

Amy Houts

# Table of Contents

# Foreword

In this book, Amy introduces the concept of American cultural diversity in a way that captures a child's interest and helps bridge their understanding of how the different cultures in America came to co-exist yet continue to celebrate their uniqueness. This has greatly helped me explain the expression referring to America as "The Great Melting Pot."

As I advanced through the pages, I found my own knowledge of American history and geography expanding. Already, this book has helped my children make a physical connection with the different geographical regions. Amazingly, they were not only able to locate the state on our map but they were able to provide a few historical facts which had been mentioned at the beginning of the chapter.

As a homeschooling family, we are always on the look-out for great science projects. As with most homeschooling families, we have quite an age range to cover, which makes science an interesting challenge. The ages span from 3 to 10 years. Amy beautifully introduced the relationship between cooking and chemistry then proceeded to lay out an experiment using popcorn. We were able to complete this project together, making age appropriate adjustments with the documentation and reporting. Science is always more fun when, upon completion, you get to eat your project!


Karen G. Heredia
Homeschooling Mom

# Introduction

In my research for this cookbook, I was awestruck by the wonderful country where I live. The fruitful plains, the fertile valleys, and the fresh and salt waters all provide an abundance of food. Because of the varying terrain, and the melting pot of people who settled here, regional areas of the United States developed distinctive dishes.

This book offers a sample of delicious recipes from our country's cooking heritage. The flavors of our American cookery are influenced by nations all over the world. Unable to include all the recipes indicative of a particular region, I concentrated on their most important food products. Making choices was difficult. It does not pretend to be all-inclusive.

You will be taken on a journey from the shores of the Atlantic Ocean, across the wide prairie, to the mountains, the Pacific Ocean, and Hawaii. Each chapter focuses on a particular region of the country. A brief geographic description of the area and activities related to that region are presented.

The selected recipes are authentic to the region, and/or to the food produced there. Clear directions are given for easy-to-make dishes, or easy versions of more difficult recipes.

The ingredients used are either in your pantry or readily available at your local grocery store. For safety, I stated what children can do, and what adults should do.

My first book in this series, **Cooking Around the Calendar With Kids - Holiday and Seasonal Food and Fun**, takes you on a journey through the year featuring favorite recipes to cook with children.

For more information about this book, visit: www.imagesunlimitedpub. com.

I collected recipes since I was a child, and began baking by myself at age twelve. Having lived in several of the regions, I was always delighted to try new local specialties.

You may have your own regional favorites you could add to this collection. I encourage you and your child to start a recipe notebook. This can be a rewarding family activity.

My hope is this book will instruct as well as entertain. Learning about the United States of America while studying food is one way of enriching your knowledge while satisfying your taste buds.

I want children as well as adults to enjoy the fun of exploring and preparing food from different regions of the United States. May these recipes become part of your cherished family favorites!

# Working Together

Working together takes cooperation; working together toward a common goal. Your common goal is completing a recipe. You can encourage children to cooperate while cooking with you by:

- explaining rules
- giving choices
- letting everyone have a turn
- acknowledging children's' needs and wants.

Cooking together is an experience everyone can enjoy when working together. Before you begin, review the safety rules and read the recipe aloud. Explain that everyone will be able to help and to eat whatever you are making when it's done.

While you are making a recipe, give children choices. For example, "Who wants to grease the pan? Who wants to measure the salt?" Each child can take a turn with a task such as stirring. Listen to each child's needs and desires. If a child says, "He stirred longer than I did," give that child another turn to stir or use a timer so it's fair.

Encourage children to complete the job they have started. It helps to give them clues related to how long the process is going to take. Saying, "We're almost done mixing and then it goes in the oven," or "Let's just wipe off the table and then we'll be done with cleanup," helps children to follow through.

# Safety Precautions

Safety is of utmost importance when cooking with children. The tasks you give children will depend on their age, ability, and maturity.

# Do's and Don'ts of Cooking Safety

## Do's

- Do: Post and review safety rules before cooking.
- Do: Wash hands before cooking.
- Do: Patiently teach children their limitations in the kitchen.
- Do: Restate a rule, or use strong words like, "Stop!" if needed.
- Do: Keep foods hot (above 140°F, 60°C) or cold (40°F, 5°C).
- Do: Use latex gloves if you (or your child) have an open cut on your hands.
- Do: Use a separate spoon when tasting food.
- Do: Allow young children to cut soft food with a butter knife.
- Do: Prevent slipping or falling by wiping up spills right after they happen.
- Do: Keep pot and pan handles turned inward so they can't be reached or knocked.
- Do: Rinse pots and pans in hot water.
- Do: Encourage children to take part in the total aspect of cooking such as: shopping, decision-making, rinsing, measuring, stirring, pouring, table-setting, and cleanup.

## Don'ts

- Don't: Allow young children to use sharp knives or kitchen scissors.
- Don't: Allow young children to use the oven.
- Don't: Allow children to use electrical gadgets like mixers, blenders, can openers.
- Don't: Use electrical appliances and gadgets near a sink or water. A deadly electric shock could happen if the electrical gadget fell in the water.

- Don't: Leave young children alone when you are cooking to answer the door or telephone.
- Don't: Allow children to lick their fingers without washing them.
- Don't: Leave refrigerated foods out for long periods of time.
- Don't: Use the same cutting board for raw and cooked food.
- Don't: Feed young children popcorn, nuts, seeds, or small foods that can cause choking.
- Don't: Serve children grapes, cherry tomatoes, or hot dogs without cutting them in half.
- Don't: Allow children to walk, run, or play while they are eating.
- Don't: Keep cleaners and plastic bags where children can reach them.

# Conserving Water, Energy, and Paper Products

We can help save our planet by being careful. Small changes can make a big difference. Run water the least amount of time possible. For example, rinse vegetables just until they are clean. Use the oven wisely. Bake potatoes and a roast at the same time. Use paper products such as plates, cups, paper towels, and napkins sparingly. A more conservative approach is to use bio-degradable "paper" products made from corn or sugarcane. Recycle cans, bottles, and paper.

# Nutrition Guidelines

Eating food that is fresh is best for both you and your children. Buying prepared food is not as healthy as cooking it yourself. Prepared food often has extra salt, fat, and sugar to make it taste better, and preservatives to keep it fresh.

Allergies plague many children today. When you bake your own bread or create a hearty soup, you know if it contains milk or peanuts, two common ingredients that cause allergic reactions. When you make food from "scratch," you know exactly what is in it.

Besides being healthier, creating your own meals is satisfying. Following are a few simple nutrition guidelines:

- Limit the amount of fat, sugar, salt, and preservatives in your family's diet.
- Take advantage of locally grown food.
- Plan to serve fresh fruits and vegetables every day.
- Include a variety of protein: lean meats, poultry, fish, beans, eggs, and nuts.
- Remember good calcium sources are milk, cheese, yogurt, sardines, salmon, spinach, and collard greens.
- Serve whole grain breads and cereals.
- Keep healthy snacks and drinks on hand in the house and the car.
- Whenever possible, cook and bake the food you eat.

# Cooking Terms

**bake:** to cook in the oven.

**batter:** a thin dough made of flour and liquid like pancake batter.

**beat:** to mix ingredients vigorously.

**bed:** the lowest layer of food as in a bed of rice under lamb kabobs.

**blend:** stir together.

**boil:** to heat liquid to the boiling point, 212°F, 100°C.

**bread:** to coat with flour, egg and bread crumbs before frying.

**brown:** cook until lightly browned.

**butter:** to spread on bread; a term used both for butter and margarine.

**carve:** to slice meat as when carving a roast.

**casserole:** a dish made with food mixed together and baked.

**chop:** to cut into pieces with a knife.

**combine:** to mix together.

**consistency:** how thick or thin.

**cream:** to beat butter and sugar for a cake.

**crimp:** to pinch together like the edges of pie dough.

**cube:** to cut into cubes.

**cut crosswise:** to cut across the width.

**cut in:** to cut butter into flour with two knives or a pastry blender for a pie crust.

**cut lengthwise:** to cut across the length.

**drain:** to remove liquid from, usually using a bowl with holes called a colander or a strainer.

**deep fry:** to fry in an inch or more of oil.

**devil:** to add spices to food like deviled eggs.

**dice:** to cut into small pieces like when dicing an onion.

**dip:** to quickly soak one food in another as when dipping bread in egg for French toast.

**discard:** throw into the garbage.

**dot:** to top with small amounts of a food as when dotting bread crumbs with butter.

**drizzle:** to drop a liquid like icing on a cake in a thin, squiggly line.

**flake:** to come apart like when fish is done cooking.

**fold:** to gently mix in a figure-eight movement as when folding blueberries into a batter.

**fry:** to cook in oil.

**grate:** to shred into small pieces with a tool called a grater.

**grease:** to rub oil, shortening, butter or margarine on the inside of a pan so the food won't stick.

**hard-boiled:** to cook until hard like hard-boiled eggs.

**harvest:** to pick fruits or vegetables when they are ready to eat.

**ingredients:** foods used in a recipe.

**knead:** to fold and turn bread dough.

**mash:** to puree with a masher as when making mashed potatoes.

**measure:** to use a container of a certain size for a specific amount of food.

**mince:** to cut really tiny pieces like when you mince garlic.

**mix:** to combine.

**pare:** to cut the peel or skin off of a fruit or vegetable, such as pare potatoes.

**pasta:** any type of macaroni or noodle.

**peel:** to take skin off of fruits or vegetables.

**pierce:** to make a small hole such as when using a fork to pierce squash before cooking.

**preheat:** to heat oven to a certain temperature before cooking food.

**prepared pan:** a pan that has been greased or made ready to be filled.

**range:** the stovetop.

**reserve:** to keep for later.

**rinse:** to run under water.

**rise:** to allow the yeast to work and make the dough larger when making bread.

**roast:** to cook meat in an oven.

**sauté:** to brown in a small amount of butter or oil.

**savory:** food for the main part of a meal, in contrast to "sweet" dessert after a meal.

**sear:** to brown quickly over high heat like when making hamburgers.

**season:** to add salt, pepper and/or herbs and spices.

**score:** to cut the surface of a food in a crisscross pattern.

**seed:** to remove the seeds.

**shuck:** to remove the shell.

**shred:** cut into strips.

**sift:** to combine dry ingredients like flour and baking powder with a tool called a sifter.

**simmer:** to cook on low heat while bubbling as when you simmer a pot of soup.

**slice:** to cut into slices.

**soak:** to let set in liquid.

**sprinkle:** to drop food on top, as when you sprinkle with chocolate chips.

**stemware:** glasses with a thin, cylindrical part to hold called a stem.

**stew:** cook together for a long time.

**stir:** to mix in a circular motion.

**stir-fry:** to cook quickly on high heat while stirring.

**stirring constantly:** to keep stirring all the time it's cooking.

**tender:** cooked until soft.

**top:** to put on top of another food.

**toss:** gently combine like when mixing salad dressing with lettuce.

**transfer:** to take food from one container to another.

**ungreased:** a pan that has not had oil or other grease rubbed on it.

**whip:** to beat air into like when whipping cream.

**whisk:** to combine using a tool called a wire whisk.

**wok:** a bowl-like frying pan used for stir-fry.

# New England

**Connecticut**
**Maine**
**Massachusetts**
**New Hampshire**
**Rhode Island**
**Vermont**

## Activities:

- Arrange a centerpiece. Place pine sprigs and fresh or dried cranberries in a glass bowl.
- Compare fresh or dried foods. Buy fresh and dried cranberries, fresh and dried grapes (raisins), fresh and dried plums (prunes). Compare their taste and texture. Which do you like better?
- Take time to daydream about a trip to New England. What state and/or city would you like to visit? Write to the Chamber of Commerce of that city or state. Ask for travel brochures. Maybe someday you will really travel there.
- Use candlelight just as people did long ago. Read a recipe by candlelight; cook by candlelight; eat by candlelight.
- Take a library trip. Check out a book from the library on the life of a lobster or other seafood.
- Prepare a typical New England meal using a few of the recipes in this chapter. Make Boston Brown Bread and Boston Baked Beans or New England Clam Chowder and Cranberry Cheese Bread. For dessert, try Boston Cream Pie or Maple Apples.

The English people who settled this rugged east coast wanted to name the land after their mother country, England. Much of New England borders the water, so fish and seafood are plentiful.

Wet, marshy areas known as bogs yield tons of cranberries. Evergreen forests cover much of the scenic mountainous land.

## Colonial America

The American colonies began in New England. At first, the "colonists," or the people who settled here, did not have enough to eat. Many of them starved. The Native Americans were very helpful in showing the people what to plant and how to survive.

The early colonists had to work very hard in order to have enough to eat. They grew fruits and vegetables, wheat to grind into flour, and herbs to season their food. They kept cattle and goats for milk, chickens for eggs, and hogs for meat. Hunting for wild game such as turkey, pheasants, and deer for their food was necessary. Meat had to be salted or cured as there was no refrigeration. Our present ham and bacon are examples of salted and cured meats.

Fruits and root vegetables were stored in a cellar to keep them over the winter months. These cellars, called "root cellars," were often only a hole dug into a hill. If the colonists worked hard and the weather was good, they had plenty to eat.

Foods were cooked over an open fire. The noon meal, often the main meal, consisted of a stew made of meat and vegetables. After the colonists learned how to plant corn, this became a plentiful and useful food product. Ground corn was made into cornmeal and baked into bread and added to other food. Corn fresh off the cob was dried and used in foods all winter.

The early settlers' pots, pans, and eating utensils were different from the ones we use today. They often shared a plate, generally made of wood. Forks and spoons were wooden, as well, or pewter. Pewter is made of tin and other metals mixed together, and looks like dull silver. Back then, pewter was popular for cups, plates, and eating utensils.

Have you ever wondered what it might have been like to be a Pilgrim? I remember one stormy night our family pretended we were Pilgrims. Our older daughter, Emily, was five years old when we decided to eat dinner by candlelight, just as the settlers probably did many times. This was a little scary for Emily, but after she became accustomed to the dimness, she said, "Oh, mommy! Isn't this pretty? But I can hardly see what I'm eating!" I asked her what she thought people used long ago to cook their food, adding there were no ovens. "A campfire," she said. I thought that was a good guess. I explained further about cooking in a pot hung in the fireplace.

# Breads

# Johnnycake Muffins

Johnnycakes were originally called "Journey Cakes," as travelers would pack them for a trip. They are made with cornmeal. In this recipe, the batter is baked into muffins. Other recipes bake Johnnycakes in a pan, like cornbread, or cook them on a griddle, like pancakes.

1 cup yellow cornmeal
⅓ cup flour
2 teaspoons baking powder
⅛ teaspoon baking soda
½ teaspoon salt
2 tablespoons sugar
1 egg
1 cup buttermilk
2 tablespoons vegetable oil

Preheat oven to 375°F. Children can place paper muffin cups in muffin pan or use shortening to grease muffin pan.

Children can help measure cornmeal, flour, baking powder, baking soda, salt, and sugar into a large bowl. Stir together with a large wooden spoon.

In a separate bowl, beat egg with a wire whisk. Measure and add buttermilk and vegetable oil to egg. Pour buttermilk mixture into the flour mixture; stir with wire whisk until just blended.

A measuring cup works well to spoon batter into prepared muffin cups; fill about ⅔ full.

Bake for 20 minutes, or until a toothpick inserted into the center of a muffin comes out clean.

Makes 12 muffins

# New England Cranberry Cheese Bread

Cranberries are a big business in New England. Did you know there is cranberry soap, cranberry tea and even a dark red glass called cranberry glass? Cranberry bread has a unique sweet and sour taste that is perfect both with a meal or for dessert.

1 orange
2 cups flour
1 cup sugar
1 ½ teaspoons baking powder
½ teaspoon baking soda
½ teaspoon salt
2 tablespoons shortening
1 ½ cups grated Cheddar cheese
1 egg, beaten
1 cup cranberries
½ cup chopped walnuts

Preheat oven to 350°F. Children can grease loaf pan, 9-by-5-by-3 inches.

Rinse and dry orange. An adult can grate orange peel by rubbing orange on a hand grater set on top of a cereal bowl. Turn and rub, turn and rub, grating only the outer peel, the orange part of the peel, as the white part is bitter. Once you have about 2 teaspoons, set aside peel. Next cut the orange in half and use a fork to remove seeds, if necessary. Squeeze orange halves to release juice into a measuring cup. Add water to measure ¾ cup. Set aside.

Children can help measure flour, sugar, baking powder, soda, salt, and orange peel into a large bowl. Cut in shortening with two knives or a pastry blender. Make a well in the center and add the orange juice mixture, cheese and egg. Stir until just mixed. Add cranberries and nuts. Stir until just mixed.

Pour batter into pan. Bake about 65 minutes, or until a wooden tooth-pick inserted in the center comes out clean. Let set in pan for 10 minutes, then remove to cool on a rack. Better if aged one day before cutting.

*Makes 1 loaf*

# Boston Brown Bread

*In colonial times, soups and stews were cooked in large pots in the fireplace. The food cooked for long periods of time. They even "baked" (actually steamed) bread in a pot, which we now call Boston Brown Bread. This hearty dark bread studded with raisins is similar to gingerbread. See the variation if you want to try baking your bread by the steaming method. Three recipes in this section begin with "Boston," as the recipes originated in this important port.*

1 cup whole wheat flour
1 cup rye flour
1 cup yellow cornmeal
1 ½ teaspoons baking soda
1 ½ teaspoons salt
2 cups buttermilk
¾ cup molasses
1 cup raisins

Preheat oven to 375° F. Grease two 8-by-4-by-½-inch or four 6-by-3-by-2-inch loaf pans.

Children can help measure all ingredients into a large bowl. Stir until just combined. Pour batter into prepared pans.

Bake 35 minutes in 8-inch pans or 25 minutes in 6-inch pans until toothpick inserted in center is nearly clean. Turn bread out of pans onto a wire rack to cool.

*Makes 2 loaves*

## Variation

**Steamed cooking method:** You will need two 1-pound metal coffee cans, tin foil, string, and a wire rack that fits in deep pan large enough to hold coffee cans when covered. (Make sure there are no sharp edges around the tops of the cans from where they were opened.) Tear off tin foil a little larger than the tops of coffee cans. Set aside.

Grease each of the coffee cans with one tablespoon shortening. Place wire rack in pan on stove. Heat water to boiling in a tea kettle or an additional pan.

Children can help mix batter and pour into coffee cans. Place tin foil over top of cans. Tie string around foil to secure. Place cans on rack in pan. Adults need to pour boiling water around cans in pan, adding enough water to come halfway up the sides of the cans. Turn heat on high. Bring to a boil and then turn heat to low. Cover and simmer for 2 hours, or until toothpick inserted in center is nearly clean. Let bread rest for 12 minutes and then turn out of pans onto a wire rack to cool.

*Makes 2 loaves*

# Blueberry Pancakes

When I was growing up, we vacationed in Maine at Rangeley Lake for a week each summer. My Aunt Jean and Uncle Morty met us there one year and we went blueberry picking. With my aunt and uncle, my parents, my sister Nancy, and I working, we had more than enough blueberries picked in a short time. Then back in our cabin we made big batches of blueberry pancakes. I still remember how delicious they were!

1 cup fresh blueberries
2 eggs, 2 cups buttermilk
¼ cup (½ stick) butter or margarine, melted
2 cups flour
2 tablespoons sugar
2 teaspoons baking powder
1 teaspoon baking soda
1 teaspoon salt

Preheat griddle on medium-high (400°F).

Children can help sort and rinse blueberries, removing any stems. Drain well. Set aside. Children can help break eggs into a large mixing bowl. Beat eggs with wire whisk or rotary beater. Children can help measure and add buttermilk, butter or margarine, flour, sugar, baking powder, baking soda, and salt. Stir until just combined. Fold in berries. Thin batter with skim, 2 percent, or whole milk, if necessary.

**Note: The griddle gets very hot. An adult should ladle the batter onto the griddle.**

Using a soup ladle, pour batter onto hot griddle in approximately 4-inch circles. Let cook a few minutes, until bubbles appear over surface of pancake. Turn and cook on the other side until brown. Repeat. Keep pancakes on a platter, covered with a cloth towel to keep warm, until all batter is used. Serve with butter and real maple syrup.

*Makes about 15 pancakes*

# Soups and Salads

# Manhattan Clam Chowder

Manhattan-style clam chowder has tomatoes.

2 dozen hard-shell clams, scrubbed
   or 2 (6.5 oz.) cans minced clams
4 strips bacon
1 onion
1 rib celery
2 carrots
3 potatoes
1 teaspoon salt
½ teaspoon thyme
¼ teaspoon dried parsley
1 bay leaf
2 cups water
1 (15 oz.) can diced tomatoes
1 tablespoon butter or margarine
1 tablespoon flour

If using fresh clams: fill soup pot with about ½-inch water. Heat to boiling over high heat. Place clams in pot. Turn down heat to medium, cover and steam 5–10 minutes, or just until clams open. Remove from heat and let cool. Once cool, adult can shuck clams (remove shell). Reserve any liquid and strain; set aside. Finely chop clams or put through medium blade of food grinder or food processor. Reserve.

Adult can dice bacon and onion. Rinse celery and trim away leaves; dice. Pare carrots and trim ends; slice. Pare and dice potatoes. Fry bacon in soup pot over medium heat until almost crisp. Add onion, and cook about 5 minutes, until tender and lightly browned. Add celery and carrots and cook 5 minutes more.

Children can measure salt, thyme, parsley and bay leaf into a small bowl. Add to pot along with potatoes, water, and tomatoes.

Adult can place pot on stove and bring to a boil. Turn down heat; cover. Let simmer until vegetables are tender, about 30 minutes. Add clams and reserved liquid.

Children can mix together softened butter or margarine and flour in a small bowl.

Adult can slowly add hot mixture to bowl, stirring to keep smooth. Add to soup and bring to a boil over medium-high heat. Turn down heat and let simmer for 5 minutes to slightly thicken. Serve immediately.

*Makes about 6 cups*

# New England Clam Chowder

New England clam chowder is creamy and has no tomatoes, unlike Manhattan-style.

2 dozen hard-shell clams, scrubbed
    or 2 (7 oz.) cans minced clams
4 strips bacon
1 onion
3 potatoes
2 teaspoons salt
½ teaspoon oregano
¼ teaspoon basil
2 cups water
2 cups milk
2 cups light cream
1 tablespoon butter or margarine
1 tablespoon flour

If using fresh clams: fill soup pot with about ½-inch water. Heat to boiling over high heat. Place clams in pot. Turn down heat to medium, cover and steam just until clams open, 5-10 minutes. Remove from heat and let cool.

Once cool, adult can shuck clams (remove shell). Reserve any liquid and strain; set aside. Finely chop clams or put through medium blade of food grinder or food processor. Reserve.

Adult can dice bacon, onion, and pare and dice potatoes. Fry bacon in a large soup pot over medium heat until almost crisp. Add onion, and cook about 5 minutes, until tender and lightly browned.

Children can measure salt, oregano, and basil into a bowl. Add to pot along with potatoes and water.

Bring to a boil. Turn down heat; cover. Let simmer until potatoes are tender, about 15 minutes. Add clams and liquid. Add milk and cream; heat, but do not boil.

Children can mix together butter or margarine and flour in a small bowl. Slowly add small amounts of hot mixture to flour/butter and mix well to prevent lumps. After it is thin and smooth, add to soup. Stir over medium heat until hot and slightly thickened. Serve immediately.

## Low-fat variation

Substitute skim milk for the milk and fat-free half-and-half for the light cream.

### Makes about 8 cups

# Clambake

Clambakes are popular in New England. First, you dig for clams in the sand. Next you dig a pit, and place large rocks in the pit. A fire is built over the rocks to heat them. Then seaweed is placed on the fire to make steam to cook the clams. The clams, wrapped in cloth, are placed on the heated rocks to cook.

# Lobster Salad

Maine is known for fresh lobsters. People eating lobster in the shell, even grown-ups, wear bibs, because it is so messy! This recipe uses the lobster meat in a salad you can eat on crackers.

**2 cups minced cooked lobster, cooled**
**⅓ cup mayonnaise**
**½ cup minced celery**
**Salt and pepper to taste**

Children can help combine all in a bowl. Serve with crackers.

*Makes 2 cups*

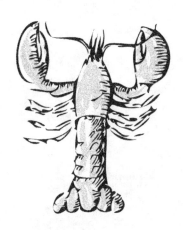

# Main Dishes/ Meats

# New England Boiled Dinner

2-3 pound corned beef brisket
4 carrots, pared
4 red potatoes, pared
2 rutabagas, pared
6 small onions, peeled
1 cabbage, cut into wedges

Children can help rinse corned beef brisket with cold water to remove excess spices and salt. Place brisket in a large pot. Add water to cover. Bring to a boil over high heat. Turn down heat to low and simmer, covered, until tender, 2–3 hours.

Remove beef from pot and place on cutting board and let it rest. Children can help prepare vegetables. Pare carrots, potatoes, and rutabagas; cut each into fourths. Remove the outer, brown layer of the onions. Place carrots, potatoes, rutabagas, and onions in pot. Bring to a boil over high heat. Turn down heat to low. Carve the beef and add the slices back into the pot. Cover and simmer about 45 minutes.

Add cabbage wedges and continue to simmer, covered, for approximately fifteen minutes until vegetables are tender. Serve beef slices and vegetables on a platter.

Serves 6.

# Creamy Turkey Casserole

Thanksgiving, with its traditional roasted turkey, began in New England when the colonists and the Native Americans celebrated the harvest. This pasta dish, made with Parmesan cheese sauce and turkey, is a perfect way to use leftover turkey.

**8-oz. thin spaghetti**
**2 cups cooked, diced turkey**
**2 tablespoons butter**
**2 tablespoons flour**
**1 ½ cups milk**
**¼ cup Parmesan cheese**
**¼ cup bread crumbs**
**1 tablespoon butter**

Preheat oven to 350°F. Grease a 2-quart casserole dish.

Cook spaghetti according to package directions, drain. Children can help measure butter, flour, and milk. To make a white sauce, an adult can melt butter in a medium-sized saucepan. Add flour and stir. Then add milk and stir constantly until boiling. Remove from heat and add cheese.

Mix turkey and spaghetti with sauce. Pour into casserole dish. Sprinkle with bread crumbs and dot with 1 tablespoon butter. Bake for 20 minutes or until hot and bubbly. Serve immediately.

## Easy variation

Substitute 1 (10-oz.) can cream of mushroom soup and ¼ cup milk for the 2 tablespoons butter, flour, and 1 ½ cups milk.

### Serves 4–6

# Shake and Bake Scallops

1 egg
1 pound fresh scallops or 1 pound package
frozen scallops, thawed
⅔ cup seasoned break crumbs
3 tablespoons butter, melted

Preheat oven to 450°F. Children can help butter a 9-by-13-by-2-inch pan.

Children can beat egg in a medium-sized bowl. Add scallops and stir until coated with egg. Measure bread crumbs and pour into a gallon-size, zip-top plastic bag. Using a slotted spoon, scoop scallops into bag with bread crumbs. Zip firmly closed. Shake gently to coat scallops with bread crumbs. Pour into prepared pan in one layer. Drizzle with butter. Bake for 15 minutes, until lightly browned.

## Variation

Peel and chop 1 small onion. Seed, rinse, and chop 1 small green pepper. Rinse and chop 1 rib celery. Sauté onion, pepper, and celery in a skillet on medium heat for 5 minutes. After drizzling breaded scallops with butter, top with vegetables. Bake as directed above.

Serves 4

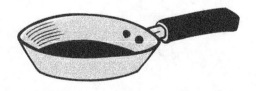

# Spaghetti Squash

*All types of squash grow in New England—summer squash (yellow and zucchini); winter squash (acorn, butternut, Hubbard, and spaghetti). Even pumpkin is a type of squash! Spaghetti squash looks like an elongated pumpkin, and is pale in color. This type of squash is fun to eat because once it's cooked, it comes apart in strands and looks like spaghetti. Serve with a spaghetti sauce.*

Children can help rinse and dry squash and place on a cookie sheet.

An adult can pierce squash with a fork or knife to let the steam escape. Bake it whole, in its skin, for about 1 hour at 375°F. Meanwhile, make sauce.

To serve, cut squash in half. Cool slightly. Children can use a spoon to help remove seeds and fibers. Use a fork or pasta server to separate strands. Serve as a main dish with sauce, or side dish with butter or margarine.

# Sauce for Spaghetti Squash

1 pound ground beef
1 onion
1 green pepper
1 (16-oz.) can tomatoes
1 (16-oz) can tomato sauce
1 (6-oz) can tomato paste
1 teaspoon sugar
1 teaspoon oregano
¼ teaspoon basil

Adult can peel and chop onion. Rinse green pepper and cut in half. An adult can chop the green pepper, after the children remove the seeds. Drain tomatoes, reserving liquid. Children can help by squeezing each tomato into the sink to release and discard the seeds. Then place on cutting board. Children can help cut up tomatoes using a butter knife.

Brown ground beef in a skillet and drain grease. Add onion and pepper and sauté a few minutes. Add chopped tomatoes, tomato sauce and tomato paste, oregano, basil, and sugar. Let simmer covered, on low, about 10 minutes to blend flavors. Serve over spaghetti squash.

## Easy variation
Cook 1 pound ground beef in skillet over medium heat. Drain grease. Add 1 (26-oz) jar spaghetti sauce. Heat and serve.

# Vegetables and Side Dishes

# Boston Baked Beans

Baked beans were among the colonists' most often-served dishes. As some of them were very strict about not working on Sunday, the Sabbath, they cooked the beans one day, and only heated them up on the Sabbath. The beans were cooked over a slow fire, or even in the ground with hot coals set under and on top of the bean pot lid.

I remember going with my family one summer to a cabin we rented in Maine. There, the owners made baked beans cooked in a pit in the ground. They let the beans cook all day. Then that evening I watched as the owner dug up the bean pot with his shovel; there were hot coals glowing all around. We and the other vacationers at the resort got to share in the delicious flavor of the beans at supper that night. I thought this was a real adventure!

Traditional Boston Baked Beans have salt pork, which gives the beans a good flavor, but bacon can be substituted.

> **1 pound dried navy beans**
> **Water**
> **¼ pound salt pork or bacon**
> **¼ cup maple syrup or molasses**
> **½ teaspoon dry mustard**

The night before, children can place beans in a 4 quart pot. Sort through and discard withered beans. Rinse beans thoroughly and drain. Cover beans with cold water, adding enough water to keep beans covered as they absorb more liquid on standing. Then let them soak overnight.

In the morning, children can help drain and rinse beans using a colander. Place beans back into pot. Add cold water to cover. Bring to a boil over high heat. Turn down heat to low and simmer, slightly covered, until beans are tender, about 1 hour. Check periodically to see that water does not boil out and beans become scorched. Also, do not cover tightly as water will boil onto the stove!

Children can test beans for tenderness: spoon out a few beans out and blow on them. The skin will start to peel if they are tender. Blow on them some more to cool them, if you plan to taste them. (However, don't put these back in the pot! Eat or discard.)

Meanwhile, fill a tea kettle or pan with water and bring to a boil. This will be used to pour over the beans before baking.

An adult should transfer the beans into an oven-safe casserole dish or bean pot. Children can add maple syrup or molasses and dry mustard. Stir. An adult should score salt pork by cutting a cross pattern with a knife. Push salt pork down into bean mixture. Pour on boiling water to cover. Bake in a 250° F oven for 8-10 hours. Check every hour or so and add more water, if needed, but do not stir.

### Serves about 6 for a meal or 10 for a side dish

### Quicker variation:

2 slices bacon
1 (16-oz.) can baked beans
3 tablespoons ketchup
1/3 cup water
1/2 teaspoon vinegar
1/2 teaspoon soy sauce
1/4 cup brown sugar
1/4 teaspoon dry mustard

Preheat oven to 300°F.

Cook bacon in a skillet or microwave. Set aside. Children can use a colander to drain and rinse beans. Pour into a casserole dish. Children can help measure and mix in remaining ingredients. Top with bacon. Bake uncovered for 1 hour.

### Serves 4-6

# Succotash

In early America, corn and beans were dried for the winter. The Native Americans used them both to cook a stew called sukquttahash. The colonists, too, were taught how to make this stew. However, they tried to make it taste better by adding milk, cream, and butter. The colonists often added potatoes, game, or chicken for a one-pot meal. The long name was shortened to succotash.

> 4 ears sweet corn or
> 1 (10-oz.) package frozen corn, cooked or
> 1 (16-oz.) can corn, drained
> 3 pounds fresh lima beans (unshelled) or
> 1 (10-oz) package, frozen baby lima
> beans, cooked or
> 1 (16-oz.) can lima beans, drained
> 2 tablespoons butter or margarine
> Salt and pepper to taste

## To prepare fresh corn:

Pick in the morning, if possible, as corn will be sweeter. (There is a saying, "two hours from field to table.") If this is not possible, then refrigerate corn. Just before cooking, children can help remove husks and silks from ears of corn. (Peel back husks from ends of corn to check for any crawly critters. If there are any, cut off the top, then continue removing husks.)

Fill a large pot of water. (Do not add salt, as salt toughens the corn.) Add 1 tablespoon each sugar and lemon juice per gallon of water and bring to a boil. Add corn. Boil 2 minutes, uncover. Remove from heat. Cover and let set 10 minutes. Remove corn to cool. Use a corn scraper or knife to remove kernels from cob.

## To prepare fresh lima beans:

Children can help rinse beans. Adults can remove the outer edge of the pod with a sharp knife. Beans will slip out of pod. Children can separate beans from pods. Discard pods.

Fill a saucepan with about 1 inch water. Add ½ teaspoon salt per cup of water. Heat to boiling. Add limas. Return to boiling, then turn down heat to medium. Simmer 5 minutes. Cover. Turn heat to low and simmer 15 minutes more or until tender. Mix corn, lima beans, butter or margarine, and salt and pepper to taste and serve.

*Serves 6-8*

## Variation:

# Creamed Succotash

2 tablespoons butter or margarine
2 tablespoons flour
1 cup milk

Children can help measure butter or margarine, flour and milk. Melt butter or margarine in a small saucepan over medium heat. Add flour; stir. Add milk gradually. Stir over medium heat until thickened but not boiling. Add to corn and bean mixture. Stir and serve.

Desserts

# Boston Creme Pie

This pie is really a two layer cake, with pudding in the middle and frosting on top. This is a fast and easy method.

1 yellow cake mix
1 (3 oz.) box instant vanilla pudding

## Chocolate Glaze:

3 tablespoons butter
1 cup powdered sugar
2 tablespoons cocoa
½ teaspoon vanilla
2 tablespoons hot water,
    approximately

Grease and flour two 9-inch round pans. Children can help measure, mix, and bake yellow cake according to package directions. Cool.

Mix vanilla pudding according to package directions. Children can spread pudding on one cake, then top with second cake.

## For glaze:

Melt butter in a pan; stir in sugar, cocoa, and vanilla. Add 1 tablespoon water, then one teaspoon at a time until the proper consistency. Spread glaze on top, letting it drip down the sides. Traditionally, the top is glazed, not the sides. Store in refrigerator.

*Makes 1 two-layer cake*

# Maple Apples

Sap is tapped from maple trees in Vermont and other Northeastern states and then boiled to make maple syrup. Once you taste real maple syrup, it's hard to be satisfied with the imitation! Here you have two products popular in this area - maple syrup and apples.

**4 baking apples** (Rome Beauty, Duchess, **or** York Imperial **are good baking types)**
½ **cup raisins (optional)**
¾ **cup maple syrup**
**2 tablespoons butter**

Preheat oven to 375°F. Children can rinse apples.

Leaving the apple whole, adult can core with an apple corer or paring knife, peel one strip of apple peel around middle of apple.

Children can place apples in a shallow pan or casserole, stuff core with raisins, and pour maple syrup over apples. Dot with butter.

Bake for 45 minutes, or until apples are soft. Adults can baste apples with syrup from pan every 10 minutes.

*Serves 4-8*

# Mid-Atlantic States

**Delaware**
**Maryland**
**New Jersey**
**New York**
**Pennsylvania**

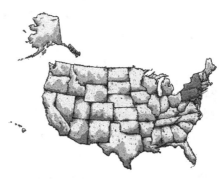

## Activities:

- Arrange a centerpiece. Children can arrange a fruit bowl of red and green grapes, pears and apples.

- Experiment with whipped cream. Buy a half pint of heavy cream. Add one tablespoon powdered sugar, if desired. Children can beat with a wire whisk or adult can beat with an electric mixer, just until soft peaks form. Careful! Don't beat too long or you will make butter. Serve over fresh fruit.

- Brainstorm apple-use ideas. Write down 10 dishes made from apples. (Hint: use the index.) To get you started: applesauce, apple pie. . .

- Research on-line. What foods did the United States presidents eat? What was the menu served for the President's Inauguration? Search "favorite foods of presidents" and other similar phrases on the internet. There are recipe books devoted to this subject.

- Use your creativity. Design a bumper sticker involving food related to the Mid-Atlantic states.

• Prepare a dish. Make some foods produced in or typical of the Mid-Atlantic states, such as Stuffed Mushrooms, Chicken Pot Pie, and Big Apple Squares, as featured in this chapter.

## Regional Description

The Mid-Atlantic states are in the *middle*, between the New England states to the north and the Southeast states to the south. They border the *Atlantic* Ocean, so they are called the Mid-Atlantic States.

New York is a mixture of city and farmland. The bustling "*Big Apple*," New York City, contrasts with picture postcard dairy farms and orchards upstate.

The Appalachian and Allegheny mountain ranges run through Pennsylvania and the Catskill mountains in New York. The nation's capital, Washington D.C., borders southern Maryland. The Atlantic coast, along with the Chesapeake Bay, provides much of the seafood harvested in the area.

Much of the nation's vegetable production is found in the Mid-Atlantic states. They grow mushrooms, cabbages, bell peppers, snap beans, spinach, tomatoes, peas and many other vegetables. These vegetables are shipped hundreds or even thousands of miles to appear in your local grocery store. New Jersey's nickname—"*The Garden State*"—fits it very well!

Americans can be very thankful for their rich and abundant selection of produce at any time of the year. The Mid-Atlantic States make a huge contribution to this abundance.

# Beverages

# Mid-Atlantic Milk Shake

Dairy farming is important to the Mid-Atlantic states as there are many large milk and cheese producers in those states.

> **1 cup milk**
> **2 tablespoons chocolate syrup**
> **2 scoops chocolate ice cream**

Measure and pour milk and syrup into blender container or deep bowl. Add ice cream. Use a blender or rotary beater to beat until smooth.

## Variation:

Chocolate Peanut Shake: Add one tablespoon peanut butter.

### Serves 1-2

# Soup, Salads, and Sandwiches

# Super Duper Easy Noodle Soup

*A surprising ingredient, tortillas, works well for noodle soup.*

2 flour tortillas
1 quart (4 cups) chicken broth OR
1 bouillon cube and 1 cup hot water

Place one tortilla at a time on a cutting board. Children can help to cut tortillas into approximately ½-inch strips using a butter knife.

Heat broth to boiling in a medium saucepan. Add tortilla strips. Turn down heat to medium and simmer 2-3 minutes or until tender. Serve in soup bowls.

## Variation:

Cook until tender: 2 carrots, pared and sliced, and 1 rib celery, chopped, in broth. Then add tortilla strips. A cup of diced chicken makes this a meal.

*Serves 4-6*

# Sunday Best Bowtie Salad with Tomatoes

Make this salad a few hours before eating to allow pasta to cool and flavors to blend.

> 1 (8-oz.) package bow tie pasta
> ½ cup olive oil or other salad oil
> ½ teaspoon basil
> ½ teaspoon oregano
> ½ teaspoon salt
> ¼ teaspoon pepper
> 2 medium-sized tomatoes
> ¼ cup grated Romano cheese

Adults can cook noodles according to package directions. Let cool. Children can measure and mix oil, basil, oregano, salt, and pepper in a small bowl or cruet. Rinse, core and chop tomatoes into bite-sized chunks. Toss with pasta in a large bowl. Refrigerate until serving time.

Serves 4–6

# Strawberry Spinach Salad

*What a pleasant blend of flavors and textures!*

1 bunch fresh spinach leaves
1 pint strawberries
1 cup walnuts
1 cup shredded Monterey Jack cheese
½ cup oil
⅓ cup sugar
¼ teaspoon salt
¼ cup red vinegar
⅛ teaspoon pepper
1 clove garlic, minced

Place spinach in a large bowl filled with cold water. Children can use their hands to stir the spinach, allowing all the grit to fall to the bottom of the bowl. Lift handfuls of spinach out of the water to drain in a colander, then dry with cloth or paper towels. Tear spinach leaves into a serving bowl, removing and discarding stem.

Rinse strawberries, remove green tops, and cut into slices about ⅛-inch thick; set aside. Preheat oven to 350°F. Place walnuts on a cookie sheet and bake for about 10 minutes, until lightly toasted.

Children can help measure oil and sugar in a medium mixing bowl. Mix with a wire whisk. Add vinegar, pepper, and garlic. Pour over spinach. Toss gently with strawberries, cheese, and nuts.

*Serves 4–6*

# Cheesy Dream Sandwiches

The ingredients for this recipe can be easily multiplied.

> **1 slice wheat bread**
> **1 tomato**
> **Cheddar cheese**

Children can place bread on a cookie sheet. Adult can broil bread on one side. Turn over. Slice tomato and cheese. Children can place a tomato slice and cheese on bread. Broil just until cheese melts.

## Makes 1 open-face sandwich

# Main Dishes/ Meats

# Hot Dog!

One of America's favorite foods is the hot dog. You can see it at baseball games, roasting on a street vendor's spit, browning at a campfire. There are "foot long" hot dogs, which are extra long, technically 12 inches or one foot long. That's a lot of hot dog! Others are skinny and some are really plump.

Hot dogs are a type of sausage, and very popular in the USA. They came from Frankfort, Germany, and were originally called Frankfurters, after the city. Some people shortened that word to "franks." In the early 1900's, a man selling frankfurters from a sidewalk stand wanted to get some attention. In order to sell more frankfurters, he called out, "Get your red hot daschund dogs!" as the long skinny sausages reminded him of the long-bodied daschund. People took out the "daschund" part and shortened this name to "hot dog." They became a big seller at the 1904 World's Fair in St. Louis, Missouri.

The Coney Island hot dog is famous in New York. Many people buy hot dogs while they walk along the ocean on the Boardwalk. The Boardwalk is a walkway made of wooden planks, along the beach. Vendors sell food and souvenirs there.

Today, the food companies that make and package hot dogs are listening to customers questioning the nutritional value in hot dogs. They are noted to be high in fat and contain chemical preservatives. Some companies are making hot dogs with other foods, such as turkey, to lower the fat content and using other ways to make them more nutritional. Before you buy hot dogs, read the label. Check the ingredients and notice how many grams of fat are in each serving.

## What's your favorite hot dog topping?

- mustard
- ketchup
- sauerkraut
- chopped sweet pickle
- sweet or hot peppers and onions
- shredded Cheddar cheese

**Note: To prevent choking in younger children, cut hot dog in half, lengthwise, before serving.**

Following are several ways of serving hot dogs. You may want to try these delicious changes.

## Pigs in a Blanket

> 1 (16-oz.) package hot dogs (8-10 dogs)
> 1 (8-oz) can crescent roll dough (8 rolls)

Preheat oven to 375°F. Work on a cookie sheet. Children can separate crescent rolls and wrap a hot dog in each. Place about an inch apart. Bake for 15 minutes or until brown.

## Chili Dogs

Make a pot of chili (see page 186) or use canned chili.

To heat hot dog: brown in a lightly oiled skillet. Toast hot dog bun to prevent it from getting soggy. Serve hot dog in bun topped with a ladle full of chili. Sprinkle with shredded Cheddar cheese, and chopped raw onion, if desired.

## Beanie Weenie

Cut hot dogs in half lengthwise and then crosswise, to make chunks. Mix with baked beans (see page 38). Bake in 350°F oven for 30 minutes until hot and bubbly.

# Stuffy Flounder

In contrast to the casual hot dog meal, try this elegant dish for a special occasion. Flounder is caught off the shores of New York state. The fillet does not have any bones. Fish, spinach and cheese are a great combination.

1 pound flounder fillets

## Stuffing:

2 tablespoons butter or margarine
1 onion
½ cup cooked, chopped spinach
1 ½ cup soft bread-crumbs
½ teaspoon salt
1 tablespoon lemon juice
½ cup grated Swiss cheese

## Sauce:

2 tablespoons butter or margarine
2 tablespoons flour
½ cup milk
½ cup chicken broth OR bouillon

Preheat oven to 375°F. Rinse fillets in cool water. Place in a glass pan, 9-by-13-by-2-inches. Pat fish dry with a paper towel. Set aside.

To make stuffing: melt butter in a skillet over medium heat. Adult can chop onion. Sauté in skillet for about 5 minutes, until soft. Children can press spinach in a colander to remove excess moisture. Add spinach, bread-crumbs, salt, lemon juice and cheese to skillet. Stir to combine. Remove from heat.

Place a spoonful of stuffing on each fillet. Let the stuffing set for a few minutes to cool slightly. Roll up fillet and secure with a toothpick. Bake for about 30 minutes or until fish flakes with a fork. Meanwhile, make sauce. Melt butter in a one-quart saucepan over medium heat. Add flour. Stir. Gradually add milk and broth and bring just to a boil, stirring frequently. Serve over fish.

*Serves 4*

# Spicy Baked Crab Meat

*Crab and other seafood dishes are popular in the states that border the coast and Chesapeake Bay. This dish is sometimes called "Deviled Crab Meat," because deviled means "spicy." Can you guess which ingredient gives this dish its spicy flavor?*

**2 tablespoons butter or margarine**
**1 small onion**
**½ cup soft bread-crumbs, divided**
**1 cup heavy cream**
**½ teaspoon dry mustard**
**½ teaspoon salt**
**¼ teaspoon cayenne pepper**
**2 egg yolks**
**1 pound lump crab meat, picked over to remove bits of shell and cartilage**

Preheat oven to 375°F.

Melt butter or margarine in a skillet on medium heat. Adult can dice onion and sauté for about 5 minutes, or until soft. Children can measure dry ingredients into small dish or cup. Wash and dry eggs. Separate egg yolks from egg whites. In order to do this, rap egg gently on a counter.

Have 2 bowls ready. Place thumbs at crack in shell, and gently pry apart, letting egg white drip into one bowl and yolk slip into the other bowl. Wash hands.

To skillet, add ¼ cup of the bread-crumbs, cream, dry mustard, salt, and cayenne pepper. Stir and heat through, but do not boil. Remove from heat and add egg yolks gradually. Gently mix in crab meat, taking care not to break up crab lumps. Spoon into crab shells or individual casserole dishes. Bake for about 10 minutes, until golden brown.

*Serves 4 to 6.*

# Pennsylvania Dutch Cooking

The Pennsylvania Dutch are not really "Dutch" at all; they are German descendants. The word "Deutsch," meaning "German," was misspelled. The two largest of these religious groups are the Amish and the Mennonites. The Amish do not use electricity, phones, or cars and farm with horses. Mennonites use electricity, phones, and cars. Both dress plainly. Both are noted for having hardworking cooks and wonderful recipes for hearty food. Following are popular Pennsylvania Dutch foods along with a few quick and easy versions.

# Chicken Pot Pie

Pot pie can be boiled or baked. When boiled, the pie crust tastes like noodle dumplings. When baked, it is a crispy, savory, main dish pie.

4 to 5 pound stewing chicken
2 teaspoons salt
¼ teaspoon pepper
1 rib celery
4 red potatoes
4 carrots
¼ cup chopped fresh parsley, or 1
    tablespoon dried

## Pot pie dough:

2 cups flour
½ teaspoon salt
1 teaspoon baking powder
2 tablespoons lard or shortening
1 egg
⅓ cup water

A stewing chicken will have a better flavor and make a better broth than a younger chicken. Rinse chicken and adult will cut up. Place in a large pot along with giblets and neck. Just cover with water. Add salt, pepper, and celery. Bring to a boil on high heat. Then turn down to low, cover and simmer for 2 ½ to 3 ½ hours, or until chicken is cooked. Remove chicken from pot. Let cool slightly. Remove meat from bone. Discard bone, giblets, neck and celery.

An adult can pare and quarter potatoes. Pare and slice carrots into 1-inch chunks. Add potatoes and carrots to pot, along with chicken and parsley. Bring to a boil. Turn down heat to low, cover and simmer for 10 minutes. Meanwhile, make pot pie dough.

Children can measure flour, salt and baking powder into a medium-sized bowl. Using a pastry blender or two dinner knives, cut in lard or shortening. Beat egg in a small bowl. Add egg and water to flour mixture and stir.

Turn out on floured pastry cloth or board. Using a rolling pin, roll out very thin. Give children a piece of their own dough to roll out. Adult can cut dough into 2-inch squares with knife or pastry wheel. Drop into boiling broth over chicken and potatoes. Turn down heat to low, cover and simmer 20 minutes.

*Serves 8*

## Easy Baked Pot Pie *Here is an acceptable alternative to pot pie made from scratch, with a good dose of homemade taste.*

Pie dough for a two-crust pie
2 cups cooked chicken
2 cups frozen or canned mixed vegetables
    (drained)
2 cups chicken gravy or 1 (10-oz.) can
cream of chicken soup plus ¼ cup water

Preheat oven to 375°F. Children can place one prepared pie crust in a 9-inch pie plate. Fill with chicken, vegetables, and gravy or soup. Make slits in top crust; place on top of filling. Using floured thumb and finger, crimp edges by pinching. Bake for 45 minutes or until browned and bubbly.

*Serves 4*

# Shaker Cooking

The Shakers, another group who came to America for religious freedom, settled in New York in 1774. They were called "Shakers" because of a dance they did during worship. They were wonderful gardeners, cooks, bakers, and preservers. Because the group was told not to eat meat during a 10 year span in the 1800's, they developed some delicious meatless dishes, which are favorites of vegetarians (non-meat eaters) today.

Following are two Shaker meatless dishes.

# Shaker Rice 'n Nut Burgers

1 cup chestnuts or slivered almonds
2 cups cooked brown or white rice
½ cup dry bread-crumbs
3 eggs
1 teaspoon dried parsley
2 tablespoons cream
2 tablespoons butter or margarine
2 tablespoons oil
Flour

If using chestnuts: prick chestnut shells and place in cold water. Bring to a boil over high heat. Cover, turn down heat and simmer for 15 minutes. Cool and chop.

Mix chestnuts or almonds, rice, bread-crumbs, 2 of the eggs, parsley and cream. Adult can heat butter or margarine and oil in a large skillet over medium heat. Beat remaining egg. Spoon a little flour onto wax paper. Children can help shape and pat mixture into 8 burgers. Dip burgers into egg and then in flour. Fry about 5 minutes on each side, until brown, turning once. Serve hot.

## Variation:
Replace almonds with cashews or pecans.

*Makes 4 servings as a main dish;*
*8 servings as a side dish.*

# Shaker Cheesy Toast

½ pound Cheddar cheese
2 cups milk
½ teaspoon salt
½ teaspoon dry mustard
Pepper to taste
4–8 slices buttered toast

Adult can dice cheese. Children can measure milk and salt into a medium-sized saucepan. Add cheese. Heat on low, stirring occasionally, until cheese is melted. Serve over toast.

Serves 4

# Vegetables / Side Dishes

# Sweet and Sour Red Cabbage

This dish has a beautiful color and tangy flavor, perfect to complement pork, chicken or beef.

2 to 2 ½ pound head of red cabbage
2 cooking apples
1 small onion
2 tablespoons butter or margarine
⅔ cup apple cider vinegar
2 tablespoons sugar
2 teaspoons salt
1 cup water
1 bay leaf
3 tablespoons grape jelly

Rinse cabbage head under cold running water. Adults can cut the cabbage into quarters on a large cutting board. Cut out the core. Use a food processor to shred cabbage, or cut crosswise into thin strips. Pare, core and slice apples. Dice onion.

Melt butter in a 4 quart pot. Add apple and onion. Cook over medium heat, stirring frequently, for about 5 minutes. Add the cabbage. Measure vinegar, sugar, salt, water, and bay leaf and add to pot. Bring to a boil over high heat. Stir. Turn down heat to very low. Cover and simmer for about 1 ½ hours, until cabbage is tender. Check to see that water has not boiled away. Add 1 tablespoon water, if needed. When done, there should be almost no liquid. Remove the bay leaf before serving.

Serves 4-6

# Mushrooms Stuffed with Sausage

Pennsylvania is the largest producer of mushrooms. Use medium to large mushrooms for this recipe, so there will be room for the sausage filling.

1 pound mushrooms (about 20)
¼ pound breakfast sausage
¼ cup shredded mozzarella cheese
2 tablespoons cup seasoned bread-crumbs

Preheat the oven to 450°F.

Rinse mushrooms by placing them in a large bowl filled with water. Swish and wash lightly by hand. The dirt will fall to the bottom of the bowl. (Do not let the mushrooms soak). Scoop out cleaned mushrooms by hand onto paper towels. Lightly sponge off. Pull out the stems. Place the mushroom caps on a cookie sheet and save the stems.

Adult can finely chop mushroom stems. Cook sausage in a skillet over medium heat, stirring occasionally, until brown and cooked through. Remove sausage from skillet. Set aside. Add the chopped stems. Cook and stir about 5 minutes, or until tender. Add the sausage, cheese and bread-crumbs. Remove from skillet; let cool slightly. With a spoon or fingers, fill mushroom caps with the sausage mixture. Bake 15 minutes. Serve hot.

## Makes about 30 stuffed mushrooms

# Desserts

# Pennsylvania Dutch Funnel Cakes

Funnel cakes are actually made using a funnel. A batter is poured through a funnel onto hot oil. The funnel is moved in a circular motion to form rings. These melt-in-your-mouth treats are popular at fairs and carnivals.

Vegetable oil
2 eggs
1 ⅓ cups milk
1 teaspoon vanilla (optional)
2 ⅔ cups flour
4 tablespoons sugar
½ teaspoon salt
1 teaspoon baking powder
2 teaspoons baking soda
Confectioners sugar

Pour oil to fill line in deep fat fryer or to the depth of at least one inch in a skillet. Preheat to 375°F; medium heat.

In medium-sized bowl, children can beat eggs; add milk and vanilla. Measure and add flour, sugar, salt, baking powder, and baking soda. Beat until smooth.

**Note: Oil gets very hot, so an adult needs to do the frying and be on hand at all times during the making of the cakes.**

Hold finger over the bottom of the funnel. Pour some batter into the funnel. Hold funnel over hot oil and allow batter to run out. Beginning in center, make swirling, circular motion, until cake is about 6 inches in diameter. Fry for about one minute, until golden brown, then turn over and fry until golden brown. Remove to drain on paper towels and immediately sprinkle heavily with confectioners' sugar. Serve warm.

### Makes about 10 cakes

# "The Big Apple" Squares

When you think of New York, do you only think of New York City? There is so much more to the state! In upstate New York, and on Long Island, bountiful fruit orchards are some of the biggest producers of not only apples but pears and grapes. These next three recipes celebrate New York state's famous products.

1 ½ cups flour
1 cup packed brown sugar
1 ½ cups oatmeal (quick cooking, uncooked)
¼ teaspoon baking soda
¼ teaspoon salt
¾ cup butter
4 apples
3 tablespoon melted butter
¾ teaspoon cinnamon
2 teaspoons lemon juice

Preheat oven to 375°F. Grease a 9-by-9-inch pan.

Measure flour, sugar, oatmeal, baking soda, and salt into a large mixing bowl. Use a pastry blender or two knives to cut in ¾ cup butter. Press half of oatmeal mixture (about 2 cups) into pan.

Adults can wash, pare, core and thinly slice apples. Mix apples with melted butter, cinnamon, and lemon juice. Place on top of oatmeal mixture. Top with remaining crumbs. Press down gently.

Bake for about 45 minutes, or until apples are tender and crumbs are golden brown.
Serve warm with vanilla ice cream.

Makes 16 squares

# Grated Apple Cookies

2 ¼ cups flour
1 teaspoon baking powder
1 teaspoon baking soda
½ teaspoon salt
¼ teaspoon cinnamon
¼ teaspoon nutmeg
½ cup butter or margarine
1 cup packed brown sugar
1 egg
¼ cup milk
2 apples, pared, cored and grated
½ cup chopped nuts

Preheat oven to 375°F. Grease a cookie sheet.

Children can measure flour, baking powder, baking soda, salt, cinnamon, and nutmeg into a large bowl; sift or stir. Set aside. In another large bowl, cream butter and brown sugar. Add egg.

Stir in dry ingredients along with milk, apples and nuts. Use two teaspoons to drop dough onto cookie sheet about 2 inches apart.

Bake for 10-12 minutes or until cookie springs back when touched. Adults can remove cookies to a cooling rack. Glaze cookies while they are warm. These cookies stay moist and keep well when stored in a cool, dry place.

## Glaze:

1 cup confectioner's sugar
1 tablespoon soft butter or margarine
1-2 teaspoons milk
½ teaspoon vanilla

Mix together all ingredients and spread on warm apple cookies.

### Makes about 6 dozen

# Honey Bear Pear Pie

4 large ripe pears
⅓ cup honey
2 teaspoons flour
Pie dough for 2 crust pie
1 tablespoon butter
¼ cup slivered almonds

Preheat oven to 425°F.

Children can line a 9-inch pie pan with prepared crust. Adult can rinse, pare, core, and slice pears. Children can mix pear slices with honey and flour and pour into pie crust. Dot with butter and sprinkle with almonds.

Cover with top crust. Make slits for steam to escape. Bake for 15 minutes; turn heat down to 350°F. for an additional 30 minutes.

*Makes 1 pie, 8 servings*

# Appalachian Highlands

Kentucky
North Carolina
Tennesee
Virginia
West Virginia

## Activities:

- Arrange a centerpiece. Children can pick wildflowers (or buy flowers) and place in a vase.
- Dress up your table. Use a quilt or a quilt top as a tablecloth.
- Count Peanuts! Count the number of peanut recipes in this book.
- Try this combination. Mix half ground turkey with ground beef next time you make hamburgers, meat loaf, or chili.
- Find the difference between a sweet potato and a yam.
- Read Early American history. Check out a book about Williamsburg, Virginia. Authentic food and dining is a focus of this restored, colonial town.
- Prepare food from the Appalachian region. Try some Chicken and Biscuit Dumplings, a Ham and Cheese Quiche, or Caramel Pecan Sticky Buns, as featured in this section.

# Regional Description

Appalachian Highlands are so named because of the main mountain range that runs diagonally through these five states of Virginia, West Virginia, North Carolina, Tennessee, and Kentucky. Virginia and North Carolina are coastal states, bordering the Chesapeake Bay and the Atlantic Ocean. Crabs and oysters are important food products in these states. Tennessee, Kentucky, and West Virginia are inland, meaning that they don't border the water or the coast.

The Appalachian Highlands are part of a huge mountain range that extends from Canada south to Alabama. In this region, the range includes: The Blue Ridge Mountains in Virginia and North Carolina, the Great Smoky Mountains in North Carolina and Tennessee, and the Cumberland Plateau in West Virginia. North Carolina claims the highest peak, Mount Mitchell.

Farms grace the fertile valleys, growing such regional favorites as peanuts, sweet potatoes, lima beans, strawberries, and tomatoes, and raising turkeys and hogs. Many people grow their own gardens and canning foods to eat year around.

# Breads

**Sally Lunn** There are two stories about this delicious bread. One is that Sally Lunn is named after an 18th century English girl of the same name, who sold the bread. The other is that the name Sally Lunn came from the French words, "soleil lune," which means sun and moon, describing the golden brown crust and the white center of the bread.

This is an easy version of Sally Lunn, using a bread machine. Or, you can mix, knead, let rise, and bake according to a traditional bread recipe. This rich dough was popular in Williamsburg: one breakfast menu includes Sally Lunn toasted. Another's luncheon faire includes the same dough but made into rolls for chicken sandwiches.

¾ cup milk
3 tablespoons shortening
1 egg
3 cups bread flour
¼ cup sugar
1 teaspoon salt
1 packet (2 ¼ teaspoons) active-dry
    yeast

Measure ingredients and add to bread machine pan in order listed. Process according to directions for white bread. Use medium bake setting.

To make and bake in a conventional oven: dissolve yeast in warm milk. Add egg, sugar and salt. Stir in half the flour, mixing until smooth. Add enough flour to make a soft dough. Turn out on flour board or cloth and knead by folding, pressing, and turning for 5 to 8 minutes.

Place in a greased bowl, turning to grease top. Cover with a cloth towel; let rise 1- 1 ½ hours, until double in bulk. Punch down. Shape into loaf and place in a greased 9-by-5-by-3-inch loaf pan. Let rise about 1 hour. Bake at 400°F for 20 minutes; turn down the heat to 350°F and bake an additional 20 to 30 minutes or until golden brown.

Note: If using bread machine, do not use "delay" setting, since raw egg and milk combinations should not set out that length of time.

*Makes 1 loaf*

# Quick Biscuits

Fresh, warm biscuits are a treat with butter and jam, or a round of spicy sausage.

2 cups flour
1 tablespoon baking powder
1 teaspoon salt
¼ cup shortening
⅔ cup milk

Preheat oven to 450°F.

Children can help measure flour, baking powder, and salt into a medium-sized bowl. Cut shortening in using a pastry blender or 2 butter knives until thoroughly mixed and mealy-looking. Add milk and stir with a fork until just combined. If too dry, add a tablespoon or two of milk to make a soft dough.

Turn dough out onto a floured tea towel or board. Children can help knead the dough by pushing with the heel of the hand, then turning and pushing. Repeat 20 times adding flour to keep the dough from sticking. With a rolling pin, roll ½ inch thick. Use a biscuit cutter or a glass to make 2-inch rounds. Dip cutter or glass in flour if sticking. Place biscuits on an ungreased cookie sheet and bake for 10-12 minutes until golden brown. Best served warm.

*Makes 12 biscuits*

# Pecans

When I lived in Memphis, Tennessee, I was invited to go pecan picking. We drove out to a huge, run- down, but still elegant-looking plantation. The pecan tree branches were wide spread, covering the yard with shade. I filled my basket with enough nuts for a pie, and some to freeze. It was a very special afternoon that I will always remember. My friend, Kay Walsh, who grew up in the south, relates an added bonus for those families who had a pecan tree in their yard:

"Pecan trees are great for swings. They grow tall with big limbs and offer lots of nice shade."

Following is one of my favorite pecan recipes. You will find another in the dessert section of this region on page 97.

# Caramel Pecan Sticky Buns

This quick and easy recipe uses biscuits from a can instead of time-consuming yeast dough. Try making it on an unhurried morning for a delectable treat. This recipe will satisfy your sweet tooth, as well as fill you up.

½ cup butter or margarine
½ cup chopped pecans
1 cup packed light brown sugar
2 tablespoon water
3 (7-oz.) cans biscuits

Preheat oven to 375°F. Grease an angel food cake pan or bundt pan.

Measure butter, pecans, brown sugar and water into a small (1 quart) saucepan. Adult can heat to boiling over high heat, stirring occasionally. Remove from heat.

Open biscuit cans. Cut each biscuit in half. Children can help roll each half into a ball. Place balls in cake pan. Drizzle caramel sauce over balls. Bake for 30 minutes, or until golden brown. An adult can place a plate on top of cake pan and turn upside-down to let the baked rolls fall on the plate. Leave the pan atop the plate for a few minutes to let all syrup drip down on buns. Take care as this is very hot. Do not let the plate slip. Serve warm.

*Makes about 10 servings*

# Soups, Salads, and Spreads

# Cream of Peanut Soup

Virginia is a big producer of peanuts. Peanuts thrive in warm climates and sandy soil. They are often found closer to the ocean. The soil in Virginia, where peanuts are grown, is usually a whitish color.

2 tablespoons butter or margarine
1 medium onion, chopped fine
2 ribs celery, chopped fine
2 tablespoons flour
1 cup peanut butter
4 cups chicken broth
1 teaspoon salt
1 cup heavy cream
Paprika
1/3 cup chopped peanuts
Bottled pepper sauce

Children can help measure all ingredients. Adult can melt butter or margarine in a large saucepan over medium heat. Add onion and celery; cook for about 5 minutes. Add flour; stir for 1 minute.

Add peanut butter. Gradually add broth and salt. Turn up heat to high and bring to a boil; stir frequently. Turn down heat to low, cover and simmer 25 minutes. Add the cream. Heat cream but do not boil. Sprinkle with paprika. Serve immediately. Pass chopped peanuts and pepper sauce at the table for garnish and flavor.

### Low-fat variation:
Use fat-free half and half for the cream.

Serves 6.

# Make Your Own Peanut Butter

Homemade peanut butter doesn't look or taste exactly like the store-bought type.

See which one you and your child like better. Ask your child, "What do you think will happen if we put these peanuts in the blender?" Discuss their predictions. After making the recipe, ask your child if his or her prediction was correct.

**1 cup blanched, roasted peanuts**
**1 to 2 tablespoons vegetable oil**
**Salt to taste**

Children can help measure and add ingredients. Use either a blender or food processor to grind the peanuts into a paste. For the blender, add only about ½ cup at a time. Add oil, then blend again until the mixture reaches spreading consistency. Add salt to taste.

Spread on crackers or bread. Enjoy! Keep refrigerated.

## Makes about 1 cup

# Crab Salad

If you are unable to buy fresh crab, substitute packaged or canned.

1 pound flaked crab
2 ribs celery, chopped fine
¼ cup onion, chopped fine
1 cup mayonnaise
½ cup mild Cheddar cheese (optional)
Pepper, to taste

Measure and mix all ingredients into a large bowl. Pour into a serving bowl. Serve with crackers, on a bed of lettuce.

Serves 4-6

# Main Dishes / Meats

# Ham and Red Eye Gravy

Lynn Kellner, in her cookbook, The Taste of Appalachia, says: "Country Ham has been the pride of Appalachia for generations. Carefully cured over hickory fires, this ham was seasoned in a smokehouse for at least a year until it was covered with a white-speckled mold. Only then was it considered ready for the table." She adds, "Some people add a couple of teaspoons of strong coffee to the gravy to give it color. Other people will tell you it's a sacrilege to do so."

1 tablespoon bacon grease or oil
1 (16-oz.) smoked ham steak
½ cup water
2 teaspoons strong coffee, if desired

Adult can heat grease or oil in a large skillet over medium heat. Fry the ham steak just until brown, about 5 minutes on each side. (Because ham is already cooked, it only needs to be heated through.) Remove the ham to a serving dish. Children can measure water and coffee. Adult can add water and coffee to the skillet, stirring to mix with pan drippings. Heat and pour over ham to serve. Good with biscuits and honey.

Serves 4

# Williamsburg

Williamsburg, Virginia is the most wonderful place in the United States of America to learn history first hand. This charming town has been restored to its colonial appearance by renovating and rebuilding many of the original structures. This huge undertaking began in 1926 by John D. Rockefeller, Jr. As the first capital of the Virginia Colony, from 1699-1776, Williamsburg boasts many political buildings, such as the Governor's Palace.

Food served in Williamsburg is authentic: dishes that appeared on tables in the 1700s of Colonial Williamsburg are served in their restaurants today. Following are some recipes I adapted from dishes served as I visited this historic town.

# Scrambled Eggs with Virginia Ham

This breakfast was one of the selections served in Colonial Williamsburg before a typical British activity: a fox hunt.

> 1 tablespoon butter or margarine
> 6 eggs
> 6 tablespoons heavy cream
> ½ cup diced Virginia ham
> ¼ teaspoon ground black pepper
> (optional)

Children can help crack and beat eggs with cream in a medium-sized bowl. Add ham. Adult can heat butter in a large skillet over low heat until melted. Add eggs and stir until eggs are just cooked. Serve immediately.

*Serves 4*

# Ham and Cheese Quiche

A "quiche" is simply a savory pie, made with eggs and cream. A variety of meats and vegetables can be substituted for the ham for a delicious light meal.

> 1 cup diced Virginia ham
> ¾ cup Parmesan cheese
> 1 ½ cups grated Swiss cheese
> 4 eggs, beaten
> 2 cups light cream
> 9-inch (1-crust) pie crust

Preheat oven to 350°F.

Measure and mix ham, cheeses, eggs, and cream. Pour into prepared pie crust. Bake 40 minutes, or until set.

Serves 6.

# Chicken 'n Biscuit Dumplings

2 tablespoons butter or margarine
3 tablespoons flour
3 cups chicken broth
1 ½ cups flour
2 teaspoons baking powder
½ teaspoon salt
3 tablespoons shortening
¾ cup milk
3 cups cooked, diced chicken

Melt butter in a large skillet over medium heat. Stir in flour. Add chicken broth gradually, beating with a wire whisk until smooth. Bring to a boil, then turn down heat to low.

For the dumplings, measure flour, baking powder, salt, and shortening into a medium-sized bowl. Use a pastry blender or 2 knives to cut shortening into flour. Add milk and stir with a fork, just until blended.

Adult can drop dumplings by spoonfuls into simmering broth. Cook 10 minutes. Then cover and cook an additional 20 minutes. Gently add chicken and heat. Serve gravy over chicken and biscuit dumplings.

*Easy variation:*
Use canned biscuits in place of the dumplings. Either cook with broth, or bake according to package directions and serve chicken and gravy on top of biscuit.

*Makes 8 dumplings*

# Seafood Cocktail Sauce

*Because Williamsburg is near the coast, there is an abundance of seafood. This sauce is great with boiled shrimp or crab, fried oysters or clams.*

1 cup ketchup
2 tablespoons fresh horseradish
or 2 tablespoons bottled horseradish
    sauce
1 teaspoon Worcestershire sauce
2 teaspoons lemon juice
1 rib celery, finely chopped

Measure and mix all ingredients into a bowl. Chill before serving. Serve as a dipping sauce with seafood. Store in refrigerator. Keeps about 2 weeks.

*Makes 1 1/4 cups*

# Vegetables and Side Dishes

# Mixed Greens

Greens are often served with fried potatoes or with cooked, dried beans such as black-eyed peas or soup beans (Great Northerns). With hot cornbread, this can be a hearty, satisfying meal in itself. Jan White, who grew up near Lake Village, Arkansas — southern Arkansas at the Mississippi border — says, the fun part is watching the greens cook:

"You will be surprised how much they 'deflate!'" A large pan of greens will cook down to a small portion. Greens need to cook only until tender or limp, but "the original idea was to put them on in the morning and they would simmer until the field hands came in for lunch. So the length of cooking time is certainly not critical."

She suggests when serving greens, to "be sure to include some of the liquid 'cause that is the 'POTLICKER' to be used as gravy over the cornbread!"

If you want to top with bacon bits or crumbled hard cooked egg, do so. Diced onions are good atop the greens, too.

**2 bunches (1 to 1 ½ pounds) fresh turnip, collard or mustard greens**
**1 cup water**
**1 thick slice of fat back or thick bacon slice**

To clean the greens and remove the stems, hold the leaf in one hand by the stem. Grip the leaf itself with the other hand and pull. The large tough stem will pull away and can be discarded. Put leaves in a large pan or clean sink. Sprinkle about a tablespoon salt on top and then fill with cold water. As you push the greens down into the water, the salt will take all "critters" and sand with it. Lift the greens from this water and place them in a pan of clean water until ready to cook them.

Adult can dice the fat back or bacon and fry in large pot or pan until browned to make at least 2 tablespoons fat. (Add oil, if needed.) Turn heat to medium. Lift a handful of greens from the water; shake to remove excess moisture and drop in grease. Careful, as it may spatter. Stir until wilted. Add another handful and repeat process until all are wilted. Add about a cup of water, cover and cook for 20 minutes or more. Serve with 'potlicker,' bacon, hard cooked egg, and onion.

*Serves 4*

# Candied Sweet Potatoes

*For an extra treat, top with marshmallows the last 5 minutes of baking.*

> **3 medium sweet potatoes**
> **2 tablespoons butter or margarine**
> **2 tablespoons packed brown sugar**
> **2 tablespoons light or dark corn syrup**

Rinse and scrub sweet potatoes with a vegetable brush; place in a large pot. Add water to cover. Add a sprinkling of salt. Adult can bring to a boil over high heat. Turn down heat to medium-low, cover and simmer until tender when pierced with a fork, about 30 minutes. Drain and cool.

Children can help peel skins from sweet potatoes and slice into chunks with a butter knife. Place in a 3-quart casserole dish. Preheat oven to 350°F.

Adult can melt butter in small saucepan. Add brown sugar and corn syrup and heat slightly until melted. Pour over sweet potatoes. Bake about 20 minutes.

*Serves 6*

# Turkeys

Turkeys are raised in the Appalachian Highlands, and production has increased in recent years. Not long ago, turkey was sold in stores only at Thanksgiving. Now, most grocery stores have it available all year. Turkey parts are sold similar to the way chicken is sold. One reason turkey is popular is because it is low in fat. It is used to lower the fat in bacon, hot dogs and sausage. You can buy it ground, too, for use in recipes substituting turkey for beef.

# Cornbread Dressing for Roasted Turkey

This recipe combines cornbread and white bread crumbs to create a dressing with a heavenly aroma and wonderful southern flavor. You can either stuff the turkey with this mixture just before roasting, or bake it in a casserole dish as directed below.

1 cup chopped celery
¼ cup finely chopped onion
¼ cup butter or margarine
Prepared cornbread, about half of
    9-by-9-inch pan
Soft white bread, about 4 slices
1 ½ cups hot chicken broth or bouillon
½ cup milk
1 teaspoon salt
2 teaspoons rubbed sage
½ teaspoon ground savory
½ teaspoon pepper
1 egg, beaten

Preheat oven to 400°F. Grease a 2-quart casserole dish.

Adult can sauté celery and onion in butter in a small skillet over medium heat until tender, about 5 minutes. Children can help crumble cornbread into a large bowl, along with enough bread cubes to make 3 ½ cups each. Add remaining ingredients; stir. (Chicken broth will be hot!)

Pour bread mixture into prepared dish. Cover and bake 20 minutes, uncover and cook an additional 10 minutes.

**Note: If you choose to stuff the turkey, remove the dressing immediately from the cavity when the turkey is cooked to prevent food-borne illness.**

Serves 8-10

# Dessert

# Pecan Bars

Child-sized portions are easy to cut in this version of pecan bars. This is similar to the traditional southern, sticky-sweet pecan pie.

1 ½ cups flour
¾ cups butter, or margarine, softened
⅓ cup powdered sugar
2 eggs
1 cup packed light brown sugar
2 tablespoons flour
½ teaspoon baking powder
½ teaspoon salt
½ teaspoon vanilla
1 cup chopped pecans

Preheat oven to 350°F.

Mix flour, butter, and powdered sugar with spoon or electric mixer. With floured fingers, using quick, light motions, press dough into a 9-by-13-by-2-inch baking pan. Bake for 15 minutes.

Meanwhile, children can help measure and mix filling. In a medium-sized bowl, beat eggs with a fork or wire whisk. Add brown sugar, baking powder, salt, vanilla, and pecans. Pour over hot crust. Return to oven and bake 20 minutes more. Cool; cut into bars.

Makes about 32 bars

# Southeast

Alabama
Arkansas
Florida
Georgia
Louisiana
Mississippi
South Carolina

## Activities:

- Arrange a centerpiece. Buy two each of white, yellow and red onions. Children can place a colorful dishtowel in a bowl. Arrange the onions in the bowl.
- Squeeze fresh orange juice for a refreshing drink. Buy Florida juice oranges. Use juicer, or simply cut in half and squeeze out the juice, catching it in a glass. Refreshing!
- Make a citrus fruit printing. Use oranges, lemons, limes, and/or grapefruit. Cut in half. Dip in paint, print on paper or cloth. Use as decoration on napkins or stationery.
- Test the "sink or float" technique. As many southern states border the Atlantic Ocean or the Gulf of Mexico, learn more about the properties of water by trying this experiment. Fill a container with water. Find a variety of heavy foods, such as carrots, potatoes, or apples, and light foods, such as pea pods, green onions,

or lettuce leaves. Drop each into the container and see whether it sinks or floats. In a separate container, pour ½ cup salt to 1 quart (4 cups) water. Do you think salt water helps to keep items afloat, or causes them to sink? Compare the sinking or floating technique in each of the water containers.

• Celebrate Mardi Gras: Mardi Gras is a New Orleans, Louisiana, celebration with parades and crazy costumes. Put on some colorful beads and get ready to celebrate with typical food from the South, such as Jambalaya or Shrimp Creole.

• Make farm animal shapes out of play dough. See recipe below.

## Let's Play Dough

This dough is lots of fun to play with, but please do not eat.

> **1 cup flour**
> **½ cup salt**
> **2 teaspoons cream of tartar**
> **1 tablespoon oil**
> **1 cup water**
> **Food coloring**

Children can help measure and pour ingredients into a medium-sized saucepan. Use a few drops of any food coloring you desire.

An adult can place pan over medium heat, stirring. Cook and stir until the mixture pulls away from the side of the pan and forms a ball. Remove from pan and let cool. Keep in an airtight container in a cool place. This play dough stays soft and pliable.

# Regional Description

These seven states, South Carolina, Georgia, Florida, Alabama, Mississippi, Arkansas, and Louisiana, are called the Southeast or Deep South states because they are in the southern and eastern half of the United States. Except for Arkansas, which borders the Mississippi River, all the Southeast states touch the Atlantic Ocean or Gulf of Mexico, with the Florida coast bordering both.

Beautiful sandy beaches line the coastal plain where fishing and seafood are popular. Forests cover large areas of the rolling hills of the south.

The Southeast states boast unique geographical formations, such as the Everglades. This is a subtropical wetland in the southern part of Florida.

Warm, mild temperatures, even in the winter, make for a long growing season. Abundant rainfall helps the crops to grow.

Rich soil produces a huge harvest of many fruits including citrus fruits, oranges, grapefruit, lemons, and limes, and peaches, watermelon, and strawberries. Vegetables are plentiful: tomatoes, cucumbers, snap and lima beans, and sweet potatoes. Other important crops are peanuts, pecans, rice, and sugarcane. The Southeast states are one of the largest producers of chickens and turkeys.

# Breads, Cereals, and Spreads

# Hush Puppies

There are differing stories about how and why hush puppies were created. My favorite is set in the American South early in the 20th century.

A common method of cooking catfish was to dip them in a cornmeal batter and fry them. Hungry dogs barked and whined when they smelled the frying catfish. In order to quiet the dogs, cooks fried spoonfuls of the cornmeal batter in the same skillet as the catfish. This cooked into delicious puffs of seasoned cornbread. To stop the barking, they threw these fried cornbread puffs to the dogs, saying "Hush, puppies."

Corn bread, spoon bread, hoe cakes, and corn dodgers are all related to hush puppies. The primary difference is the cooking method.

We think hush puppies are too good to feed only to puppies.

1 cup cornmeal
2 tablespoons flour
¼ teaspoon baking soda
¼ teaspoon salt
1 egg, beaten
¾ cup buttermilk
3 tablespoons finely chopped onion
      (optional)
Oil

Children can help measure and mix cornmeal, flour, baking soda and salt into a large bowl. Make a well in the center and add the egg, buttermilk, and onion. Stir until just combined.

In a large skillet, pour oil to the depth of about ½ inch. Heat on medium.

**Note: oil gets very hot. An adult should fry the Hush Puppies.**

Drop spoonfuls of batter into hot oil in skillet. Fry until golden, turn and fry for a total of about 5 minutes. Remove from oil and drain on paper towels. Serve warm.

Makes about 2 dozen

# Goober Bread

This bread is made with peanut butter. Other names for peanuts are goobers or goober peas, hence the name of the bread. Peanuts are a kind of pea, or an edible seed of a legume, and not really a nut. Almost half of all peanuts produced in the United States are grown within 100 miles of Dothan, Alabama, home of the National Peanut Festival.

**2 cups flour**
**⅓ cup sugar**
**2 teaspoons baking powder**
**1 teaspoon salt**
**1 egg**
**1 cup milk**
**¾ cup chunky peanut butter**

Preheat oven to 350°F. Grease a 9-by-5-by-3-inch loaf pan.

Children can help measure flour, sugar, baking powder and salt into a large bowl. Sift or stir to combine. Make a well in the center and add egg, milk and peanut butter. Take turns stirring with a fork until combined.

Pour batter into loaf pan. Bake about 50 minutes. Let set 10 minutes. Turn out of pan, and let cool completely on rack. Slice and serve with butter.

Makes 1 loaf

# Cheese Grits

Grits are a Native American corn-based food much like a thick porridge or polenta. It is common to the Southern United States and is traditionally served for breakfast. It is found in the cereal section of the grocery store and is similar in appearance to other cooked cereals. Plain grits are good for breakfast, but this cheesy grits casserole is perfect for brunch, lunch, or supper. It's particularly good with ham, bacon, or sausage.

4 cups water
½ teaspoon salt
1 cup quick-cooking grits
1 ½ cups grated sharp Cheddar cheese
¼ lb. block package of processed
    American cheese, cut into chunks
2 tablespoons butter or margarine
½ teaspoon garlic powder
2 eggs

Preheat oven to 350°F. Children can grease a 2-quart casserole dish.

Measure water and salt into a medium-sized pan. Adult can bring to boil over high heat and slowly add grits, stirring constantly. Reduce heat to low. Simmer 5 minutes, stirring occasionally. Remove from heat.

Add cheeses, butter and garlic powder to pan; stir until cheese is melted. Children can beat eggs in a small bowl. Adult can stir a small amount of hot grits mixture into eggs. Stirring constantly, slowly pour egg mixture back into pan. Pour into prepared casserole dish.

Cover and bake for 35 minutes. Uncover and bake an additional 10 minutes. Let stand 5 minutes before serving.

Serves 8-10

The following recipes go well with toast, waffles, French toast, or other breakfast-type dishes.

# Florida ☆ Orange Syrup

½ cup (1 stick) butter or margarine
½ cup sugar
⅓ cup (half 6-oz. can) frozen orange
    juice concentrate

Children can help measure butter, sugar, and orange juice concentrate into a small (1 quart) saucepan. Adult can cook and stir orange mixture over low heat until butter is melted. Do not boil.

Remove from heat. Let cool 10 minutes. Children can use a rotary (hand) beater or wire whisk to beat until slightly thickened. Serve warm over pancakes, waffles, or French toast.

# Easy Peach Freezer Jam

The soft, fuzzy, blushing peach is grown in abundance in South Carolina and Georgia.

4 ripe peaches (3 cups mashed)
3 tablespoons lemon juice
4 cups sugar
1 (1 ¾ oz.) package powdered pectin
1 cup water

Adult needs to scald the peaches to remove the skins. This is done by lowering peaches with a slotted spoon into hot, boiling water for approximately 1 minute or until skins begin to loosen. Cool. Slip skins off peaches and cut each in half. Remove pit. Children can cut peaches into thin slices, using a butter knife. Place in heatproof bowl. Add lemon juice. Children can crush fruit, releasing the juice by using a potato masher or fork or swirl in food processor. Amount should measure about 3 cups. Stir in sugar. Let set for 20 minutes, stirring every 5 minutes.

Children can pour pectin into a small saucepan. Add water; stir. Adult can bring pectin mixture to a boil over high heat, then turn down to low. Boil and stir one minute. Pour hot mixture over peaches. Stir for 2 minutes. Then pour into 4 or 5 half pint (1 cup) jars leaving about ½ inch at the top, as the jam will expand when freezing. Wipe off rim of jars and attach lids. Let stand until jam is set, about 1 hour. Then refrigerate or freeze. Keeps about a month in refrigerator or 6 months in freezer.

*Makes about 4 cups*

# Soup and Sandwiches

# Fresh Tomato Soup

With its warm weather and long growing season, the Southeast is a top producer of tomatoes.

4 cups of fresh tomatoes
1 slice of onion
2 cups chicken or beef broth, or water
    plus 3 bouillon cubes
4 whole cloves
2 teaspoons sugar
1 teaspoon salt
2 tablespoons butter or margarine
2 tablespoons flour

Adult needs to scald the tomatoes to remove the skins. First, remove core and score bottom with an X. Then cook tomatoes in a pot of boiling water for approximately 2 minutes or until skins begin to loosen. Remove with a slotted spoon into ice water. Cool. Slip skins off tomatoes, squeeze to remove seeds; discard seeds. Dice tomatoes and onion.

Children can help measure and add ingredients. Combine tomatoes, onion, water, cloves, sugar and salt in large pot. Adult can bring mixture to a boil. Turn down heat to low and simmer 20 minutes. Put through a strainer to remove tomato peel and cloves, and to make a pureed consistency. Return to pot and place on medium heat.

In a small saucepan, melt butter over medium heat; add flour and stir 1 minute. Whisk the butter mixture into the soup, a little at a time. Bring to a boil to thicken, and serve.

*Makes 4 cups*

# Glorified Peanut Butter Sandwich

Amounts for one sandwich:

2 slices whole wheat bread
Approximately: 2 tablespoons peanut
    butter
2 teaspoons jelly or honey
10 raisins
2 tablespoons grated carrot
6 slices banana

Children can spread peanut butter on bread. Assemble by adding choice
of jelly, honey, raisins, grated carrot and sliced banana. Top with second
slice of bread.  Cut in half or quarter, if desired.

# Orange-Honey Chicken Sandwiches

This dish combines the sweet flavor of oranges and honey. Florida is the biggest producer
of oranges and a major producer of other citrus fruits such as grapefruit, lemons, and
limes. Some are eaten fresh while others are frozen for juice or used in other foods. The
southeast region is also one of the largest producers of chicken. The chicken for this
recipe can be grilled outside or broiled in the oven.

⅓ cup (½ of a 6-oz. can) frozen orange
juice concentrate
2 tablespoons soy sauce
2 tablespoons honey
1 teaspoon ground ginger
4 boneless, skinless chicken breast halves
4 hamburger buns
Salt and pepper
Mayonnaise
Red leaf lettuce

Children can help measure and mix orange juice, soy sauce, honey, and ginger in a casserole dish. This marinade can be made early in the day or the night before.

Rinse chicken; pat dry and arrange in casserole dish. Pour marinade over chicken. Cover and set in refrigerator for at least an hour or longer before grilling.

About 15 minutes before mealtime: If grilling, adult can grill chicken over medium coals for 6 minutes. Turn chicken and brush with marinade. Cook 6 minutes more, or until chicken is cooked through. Discard remaining marinade. If broiling, follow directions below.

To broil: Place chicken in a broiler pan. Adult can broil chicken close to heat for 5 minutes. Turn and brush with marinade. Broil an additional 5 minutes, or until chicken is cooked through.

Toast buns on grill or in toaster. Sprinkle with salt and pepper to taste. Serve chicken on buns with mayonnaise and lettuce.

*Serves 4*

# Main Dishes/ Meats

# Biscuits and Gravy

> 1 can biscuits
> 1 pound breakfast sausage
> 4 tablespoons flour
> 2 cups milk (or half water)
> Salt and pepper to taste

Children can place biscuits on cookie sheet. Bake according to package directions.

Meanwhile, cook sausage in a large skillet over medium, separating into chunks with a fork or pancake turner. When sausage is cooked through, drain all but about 2 tablespoons grease. Remove sausage from pan and set aside.

Children can help measure flour; add to skillet. Stir until combined and bubbly. Add milk gradually, stirring until thickened. Return sausage to pan and heat through. Serve immediately over split, hot biscuits.

## Serves 4

# Red Beans and Rice

Red beans are one of Louisiana's famous dishes. When I was a teenager living in St. Louis, my good friend from Louisiana, Carol Martin, had Red Beans and Rice every Sunday for dinner.

> 1 cup dried red beans
> Water to cover
> 3 tablespoons bacon drippings or oil
> 1 cup finely chopped onion
> 1 cup finely chopped celery
> 1 cup white or brown rice

Children can rinse and sort through beans, discarding any questionable ones. Observe how hard the beans are before they are cooked. (These are the same types of beans used in "bean bags" and bean-stuffed animals.)

Measure beans and water into a large pot. Either soak beans overnight, or boil for 2 minutes and let set for 2 hours. Then drain, whether you use the overnight or quick method. Add fresh water to cover.

Sauté onion and celery in bacon drippings or oil. Add to beans. Bring to a boil, turn down to low, cover, and simmer about 1 hour, or until tender. Meanwhile, cook rice according to package directions. Serve beans over hot, fluffy rice.

*Serves 4–6*

# Fried Chicken Tenders

¼ cup (½ stick) butter or margarine
1-pound package boneless chicken tenders
¼ cup milk, approximately
¼ cup flour, approximately
Salt and pepper to taste
Bottled Ranch salad dressing

Heat butter or margarine in a large skillet over medium heat. Children can help rinse chicken tenders, pat dry with paper towel.

Scoop about ¼ cup flour onto a piece of waxed paper. Season flour with salt and pepper. Dip chicken in milk, then in flour. Add more flour, salt and pepper, if needed. (Discard flour when recipe is completed.)

Adult can fry about 5 minutes on each side, or until browned and cooked through. Serve with Ranch dressing.

*Serves 4*

# A Creole Memory

My friend Margaret Preus grew up in New Orleans, Louisiana. She lived four blocks from Lake Pontchartrain. Her mother would give her $20 to ride her bike to the house of her hairdresser whose husband did some shrimping.

"The lady would weigh out 20 lbs. of shrimp kept in ice water (caught that morning)," says Margaret, "and I would ride home with it in my bike basket. My mother would keep half gallon milk cartons and pour the shrimp and water into those and freeze them. We would eat on this shrimp, either boiled for 5 min. in crab boil, chilled, then served with a sauce (ketchup, lemon juice, and horseradish ) or as a shrimp creole on rice. Yumm!"

# Shrimp Creole

Creole cooking is a mixture of French and Spanish cooking, originating in New Orleans. This delicious, spicy, versatile sauce can be mixed with boiled shrimp, as in this recipe, or with chunks of cooked, boned chicken and served over a bed of rice. It can also be poured over an omelet.

2 tablespoons butter or margarine
1 onion
1 green pepper
2 cloves garlic
2 (14 ½-oz.) cans diced tomatoes
¼ cup chopped fresh parsley or 1
    tablespoon dried 2 bay leaves
½ teaspoon thyme
¼ teaspoon salt
⅛ teaspoon sugar
1 tablespoon cornstarch
¼ cup water
½ teaspoon hot pepper sauce
1 pound raw shrimp

Melt butter in a large skillet over medium heat. Adult can cut onion and green pepper in half. Children can remove onion skin and pepper seeds. Adult can chop onion and green pepper. Sauté until soft, 5-10 minutes.

Meanwhile, adult can mince garlic. Add garlic. Sauté 1 minute more. Add tomatoes. Children can help measure parsley, bay leaves, thyme, salt, and sugar. Stir into tomato mixture, bring to a boil, then turn down to low, cover and simmer 15 minutes. Combine cornstarch, water, and pepper sauce. Add to skillet, stir, and simmer until mixture thickens slightly. Remove bay leaves.

Meanwhile, use the tip of a small knife or deveiner to remove the black vein from the shrimp; then peel shell. Add shrimp to pot and simmer for 10 minutes. (Don't overcook shrimp or they dry out and taste tough.) Serve over rice. **Note: The sauce freezes well.**

Serves 4

# Jambalaya

This dish has the same tomato base as Creole, with ham as the main ingredient. "Jambalaya" is a Creole name from the French word jambon, meaning "ham."

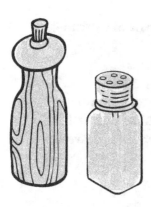

1 tablespoon oil
1 pound ham or Polish sausage
1 boned, skinned chicken breast, cut
    into pieces
1 onion
1 green pepper
1 rib celery
1 (14 ½-oz.) can diced tomatoes
½ teaspoon salt
1 teaspoon hot pepper sauce
1 tablespoon chopped fresh parsley
3 cups cooked rice (1 cup uncooked)

Heat oil in a large skillet over medium heat.

Adult can dice ham into ½-inch cubes, or cut Polish sausage lengthwise and then crosswise into ½-inch chunks. Add ham or sausage to skillet and sauté until lightly browned, about 5 minutes, adding 1 more tablespoon of oil to pan, if needed. Remove ham and add chicken breast and sauté until cooked through, about 5 minutes. Remove meats and set aside.

Cut onion and green pepper in half. Child can remove onion skin, pepper seeds, and break celery rib off stalk. Adult can chop onion, green pepper, and celery. Sauté until soft, 5-10 minutes.

Meanwhile, make rice according to package directions. Children can help measure rice, water, salt, and butter into a saucepan.

Return ham and chicken to skillet, along with tomatoes, salt, and pepper sauce. Bring to a boil, turn down heat to low and simmer for about 10 minutes. Sprinkle with parsley. Serve over hot, fluffy rice.

*Serves* 4

# Brunswick Stew

Brunswick stew is popular in the Southeast. A variety of vegetables can be added, whatever is available.

1 small onion, chopped
2 slices bacon
1 (15-oz.) can diced tomatoes
2 cups pared, diced potatoes
1 cup frozen baby lima beans
3-4 cups chicken broth or bouillon
2 cups diced, cooked chicken
1 cup frozen corn or corn kernels
   from 4 ears sweet corn
1 teaspoon Worcestershire sauce

Adult can cut up vegetables. Children can help measure ingredients.

Fry bacon until crisp in a large pot. Add onion and cook until soft, about 5 minutes. Add tomatoes, potatoes, lima beans, and chicken broth.

Bring to a boil over high heat; turn down to low, cover and simmer 45 minutes. Add chicken, corn, and Worcestershire. Simmer 10 minutes more. Serve in bowls.

Serves 4

# Vegetables/Side Dishes

# Tomato Butterfly

Here is an interesting way to enjoy fresh tomatoes.

- Adult can cut a slice of tomato; cut slice in half
- Children can place halves back-to-back, rounded sides touching
- Decorate "wings" with sliced green or black olives
- For antennae, place chives between "wings"

# Deviled Eggs

A warm weather favorite, deviled eggs get their name from the spicy mustard that is mashed with the yolks and placed back into the bowl of the egg white. This gives the bland, hard-cooked egg a distinctive look and flavor.

6 eggs
½ teaspoon salt
½ teaspoon dry mustard
3 tablespoons mayonnaise
Dash of pepper
Dash of paprika

**To hard-cook eggs:** children can carefully place eggs in a single layer in a saucepan. Add enough cold water to completely cover eggs. Partially cover pan with lid and bring to a rolling boil. Adult must remove pan from heat and fully cover pan with lid. Let eggs stand in the hot water 18-20 minutes. Adult must pour off hot water, or use slotted spoon to move eggs into another bowl. Run cold water over eggs. Refrigerate until thoroughly cooled.

Kids will enjoy rolling and cracking egg shell; peel. Discard shell and rinse eggs in cold water, getting rid of all egg shells. Cut in half lengthwise. Slip out yolks into a mixing bowl. Mash with a fork or potato masher. Mix in salt, mustard and mayonnaise. Spoon yolk mixture back into egg white, dividing the mixture evenly among all the egg whites. Dust with pepper and paprika. Cover and refrigerate until ready to use.

## Makes 12 deviled eggs

# Desserts

# Easy Rice Pudding

Long grain rice is grown in the Southeast. Arkansas, Louisiana, and Mississippi are the top three U.S. producers.

> 1 package instant vanilla pudding
> 2 cups cooked brown or white rice
> ½ cup raisins

Children can help measure and mix pudding according to package directions. Stir in rice and raisins. Refrigerate until ready to serve.

*Makes 4–6 servings*

# Buttermilk Pie

This delicious custard pie recipe, from Cindy Brown, who is originally from Jonesboro, Arkansas, was handed down from her mother. The buttermilk gives it a distinctive flavor.

> 3 eggs
> 2 cups sugar (less ½ cup if preferred)
> ¼ cup melted butter
> 1 cup buttermilk
> 3 heaping tablespoons flour
> 1 teaspoon vanilla or
>     ¼ teaspoon nutmeg, if desired
> 9" unbaked, deep pie shell

Children can help measure and mix ingredients until well blended.

Pour into 9-inch pie shell and bake at 350°F approximately 50 minutes. Pie will be golden brown.

*Serves 6*

# Great Lakes

Illinois
Indiana
Michigan
Minnesota
Ohio
Wisconsin

## Activities:

- Arrange a centerpiece. Children can arrange slices of cheese and a variety of crackers on a tea towel in a basket.
- Visit the grocery store. Observe different sizes, shapes, colors, and names of cheeses at the grocery store. Buy a type of cheese you haven't eaten before.
- Make cheese cutouts. Use cookie cutters to make shapes out of sliced cheese and use for open-faced sandwiches.
- Create cheese sculptures. Using a butter knife, whittle away at a chunk of cheese to make animals, geometric shapes, or modern design sculptures. Use on crackers with soup for lunch.
- Concoct ice cream sundaes. Everyone makes their own ice cream sundaes. Supply toppings, such as nuts, chocolate syrup, and cherries.
- Compare rice products. Compare three types of rice: white, brown, and wild, before and after cooking. Which one do you like best?

# Regional Description

To the north, these states border four of the Great Lakes: Lake Erie, Lake Huron, Lake Michigan, and Lake Superior. In fact, water is a vital part of their history, economy, and culture. Minnesota has more than 15,000 lakes. Two main rivers, the Mississippi and the Ohio, border these six states.

The Great Lakes region is known for its famous dairy products: milk, cheese, and butter. Rich, black soil produces many fruits and vegetables. Oats, corn, soybeans, peas, cucumbers, cherries, and cranberries are among the chief food crops. These states are also producers of hogs, turkeys, chickens, and eggs.

Michigan's orchards produce bountiful harvests. It is the number one producer of tart cherries, cranberries, and close to number one in apples and sweet cherries. Johnny Appleseed planted apple seeds throughout this region.

Wisconsin and Minnesota are major producers of milk, cheeses, and butter. Big dairy farms produce the milk and cream needed for these products. While there are several breeds of cows of different colors, the largest milk producer, the Holstein, is the well-known black and white color.

# Butter

Did you hear the story about the two frogs, each caught in a crock of cream? One frog just sat there, "It's hopeless to try and get out," he said, and he drowned. The other frog struggled and jumped and splashed until the cream turned into butter and he climbed out. The moral is: don't give up, keep trying and something wonderfully unexpected will happen.

There is nothing like the taste of butter when you spread it on bread. Cookies, cakes, pies, and candies are richer and more flavorful when butter is used in the recipe. Making butter is a learning experience, and it's fun! Following is an easy way for you and your children to produce a small amount of butter in a short time.

# Handmade Butter

½ pint heavy cream
Salt, to taste

Pour cream into a small container with a lid, such as a baby food jar, one fourth full. Each child should have his or her own container. Children can shake containers until cream thickens into butter, about 5 to 10 minutes.

Music makes this activity fun (see below). Notice the changes in the cream: first it will become thick and cling to the sides of the jar, creating whipped cream. Then all of a sudden, a liquid will separate from a solid, creating butter. Pour off the liquid and lightly sprinkle butter with salt. Children can spread the butter on bread.

## Butter Song

To the tune of "Row, Row, Row Your Boat"

Shake, shake, shake the cream
Gently up and down,
Shake, shake, shake, shake
Butter for our bread!
(repeat)

# Breads

# Cheese Biscuits

2 cups flour
1 tablespoon baking powder
1 teaspoon salt
¼ cup butter
¾ cup milk
1 cup grated sharp Cheddar cheese

Preheat oven to 450°F.

Children can help measure flour, baking powder, and salt into a large bowl. Cut in butter with a pastry blender or two butter knives until it resembles meal. Use a fork to stir in the milk and cheese. Gather dough and place on floured cloth or board.

Children can help knead dough by folding and turning a quarter turn about 25 times. Use a rolling pin to roll ½-inch thick. Cut into 2-inch rounds with floured biscuit cutter or drinking glass. Place on ungreased baking sheet. Bake about 10 minutes, or until golden brown. Serve warm or cold.

*Makes 1 dozen biscuits*

# Wild Cat Muffins

Wild rice is grown in the Great Lakes area. It is a seed from a grass and is difficult to harvest.

5 tablespoons melted butter
2 eggs
1 cup cooked wild rice
1 cup milk
1 ½ cups flour
2 teaspoons sugar
3 teaspoons baking powder
½ teaspoon salt

Preheat oven to 400°F. Use a 12 cup muffin pan. Place paper muffin cups in pan, or grease or spray pan.

Melt butter. Set aside. Children can help beat eggs in a medium-sized bowl; add rice, milk, and butter. Sift flour, sugar, baking powder, and salt into batter; stir lightly, just until mixed. Spoon batter into muffin cups. Bake for 25 minutes or until lightly browned.

## Makes 12 muffins

# No-Knead Dilly Bread

This bread smells wonderful! The cheese gives it a hearty, rich texture. Another plus is that this bread requires no kneading; just mix, let rise, and bake.

2/3 cup warm water
1 package (2 1/4 teaspoons) active-dry yeast
1 cup cottage cheese
1 tablespoon butter
2 tablespoons sugar
1 tablespoon dried, minced onion
1 1/2 teaspoons dill seed
1 teaspoon salt
1/4 teaspoon baking soda
1 egg
2 1/4 cups flour
Sesame seeds

Pour water into a large bowl. Test the temperature by dipping your finger in the water; it should not feel hot at all, but warmer than lukewarm. Add the yeast; stir until it is dissolved. Children can help measure and add the cottage cheese, butter, sugar, onion, dill seed, salt, baking soda, and egg. Stir to combine. Add flour to make a soft dough, blending well.

Leave the dough in the bowl, cover with a dish towel and let rise 1 to 1 1/2 hours. Children can punch down dough. Grease a 1 1/2 quart casserole dish. Turn dough into casserole dish. Let rise 1 hour. Preheat oven to 350°F. Bake 40 minutes. Turn out of casserole dish onto wire rack to cool. Brush with butter, and sprinkle with sesame seeds, and salt. Serve warm or cold. Great toasted.

*Makes one loaf*

# Soups and Salads

# Wild Rice 'n Cheese Soup

*A great way to use leftover wild rice.*

4 medium potatoes, pared, diced
1 cup wild rice
½ lb. fresh mushrooms, sliced
¼ lb. Canadian bacon, cut in ½ inch pieces
1 large onion, chopped
1 clove garlic, minced
1 tablespoon butter or margarine
2 tablespoons flour
2 cups milk
1 ½ cups chicken broth or bouillon
1 (5 oz.) jar Old English cheese spread
½ tsp. salt
¼ tsp. white pepper

Prepare potatoes. Place in a medium-sized pot. Cover with cold water. Heat over high heat until boiling. Then turn down to low. Simmer until tender, about 10-15 minutes. Set aside. Show children wild, brown, and white rice. Discuss and compare how they are alike and how they are different. Cook wild rice according to package directions. Set aside.

Children can help slice mushrooms with a butter knife. Adult can prepare onion and garlic. Melt butter or margarine over medium heat in a large pot. Add mushrooms, bacon, onion, and garlic. Sauté until onion is soft, about 10 minutes.

Add flour; cook, and stir for 1 minute. Add milk and chicken broth. Cook over low, stirring occasionally, until soup is slightly thickened, about 15 minutes. Drain potatoes. Add to soup along with rice, cheese, salt and pepper. Stir until cheese is melted. Serve immediately.

*Serves 8*

# Cucumber Salad

Farms and orchards cover the fields of the Great Lake states, giving us an abundance of fruits and vegetables.

**1 medium-sized cucumber**
**Salt**
**Bottled Italian salad dressing**

Rinse and pare cucumber. Using a cutting board, cut crosswise into ¼-inch slices. Place circles of cucumbers side-by-side on cutting board. Children can gently sprinkle salt on cucumbers. Let set 10 minutes. Blot with a white paper towel, turn over and sprinkle with salt. Let set 10 minutes. Blot with paper towel. Place in a serving bowl and pour on Italian dressing. Stir. Refrigerate until ready to serve. Keeps for several days.

*Serves 4*

# Main Dishes/ Meats

# Cheese Omelet

2 eggs
1 tablespoon butter
¼ cup grated Cheddar cheese

Melt butter in a small skillet over medium-high heat, being careful not to let butter burn. Children can help crack and beat the eggs in a bowl. Add to skillet. Stir eggs once with pancake turner, then slide skillet over burner to cook eggs quickly and evenly. Turn, sprinkle with cheese, fold over, and serve immediately.

## Makes 1 omelet

# Cheesy Noodle Casserole

1 (8-oz.) package noodles
1 pound lean ground beef
1 teaspoon salt
⅛ teaspoon black pepper
¼ teaspoon garlic salt
1 (8-oz.) can tomato sauce
1 cup cottage cheese
1 cup sour cream
1 cup chopped green onions
1 cup grated sharp Cheddar cheese

Preheat oven to 350°F. Grease a 2-quart casserole dish.

Cook noodles according to package directions; rinse in cold water and drain. Brown beef in a skillet over medium heat; drain grease. Add salt, pepper, garlic salt, and tomato sauce to skillet. Simmer 5 minutes. Children can help measure and combine cottage cheese, sour cream, onions, and noodles in a large bowl.

Layer noodle mixture and meat mixture in casserole dish. Top with Cheddar cheese. Bake for 20 to 25 minutes or until cheese is melted and lightly browned.

*Serves 4–6*

## Pasties

A "pasty" (pronounced pass-tee) is a wonderful meat and potato turnover. Around 1850, the Cornish miners introduced pasties to the Lake Superior area from Cornwall, England. The miners in Michigan and Minnesota often brought this scrumptious, satisfying "meal in a pastry" for their lunch.

> 2 cups flour
> 2/3 cup butter, shortening or lard
> 1 teaspoon salt
> Approximately 1/3 cup cold water
> 1 pound sirloin steak, cut into 1/4-inch cubes
> 2 medium potatoes, pared and chopped
> 1 rutabaga (optional)
> 1 onion, chopped fine
> 1 carrot, sliced
> Salt and pepper to taste

Children can help to prepare pastry dough by measuring flour and salt into a medium-sized bowl. Cut in butter or other shortening with a pastry blender or two butter knives until it resembles meal. Use a fork to stir in the water. Gather dough and place in refrigerator while preparing filling.

Preheat oven to 350°F. Adult can cut meat and vegetables and mix together in a bowl. Add seasoning. Place pastry dough on floured cloth or board; divide pastry into 4 pieces. Children can help roll each piece of dough into an 8-inch circle about ¼-inch thick. Place on a greased cookie sheet.

Spoon a fourth of the meat mixture onto each circle of dough. Gently pull pastry over meat mixture and seal by pinching together or pressing edges with fork. Cut 2 slits in each pasty to allow the steam from baking to escape. Bake for about 1 hour or until meat and vegetables are cooked and pastry is golden brown. Eat hot or cold.

### Makes 4-8 pasties

# Meat Loaf with Zesty Topping

1 ½ pounds ground beef
¼ medium onion, minced
2 slices dry toast, cubed
¾ cup applesauce
1 teaspoon salt
¼ teaspoon pepper
2 tablespoons catsup
2 tablespoons brown sugar
1 teaspoon dry mustard
1 teaspoon prepared horseradish

Children can help measure and mix ground beef, onion, bread cubes, applesauce, salt, and pepper. Pack into a 9-by-5-by-3-inch, greased loaf pan. Combine catsup, brown sugar, mustard, and horseradish; spoon over top of loaf. Bake at 325°F for 1 hour.

*Serves 6*

# Pork Chops with Cranberry Sauce

> 1 tablespoon butter or margarine
> 4 pork chops
> Salt and pepper
> Half of 1 (16-oz.) can whole berry
>     cranberry sauce OR use fresh
>     cranberry sauce recipe

Heat butter in a large skillet over medium heat. Brown pork chops, turning once. Season with salt and pepper. Children can help measure half of cranberry sauce; add to skillet. Cover, turn down to low. Simmer 45 minutes or until chops are thoroughly cooked. Serve with sauce.

*Serves 4*

# Cranberry Sauce

**Variation.** Substitute fresh cranberries when they are in season for canned cranberry sauce above.

> **1 cup fresh cranberries**
> **¼ cup brown sugar**
> **2 teaspoons cornstarch**
> **⅔ cup cold water**

Children can measure cranberries and brown sugar in medium saucepan. Measure and mix cornstarch and water and pour in saucepan. Adult can turn up heat to medium. Stir until sauce is thickened. Pour sauce over chops. Serve.

Serves 6.

# Vegetables/Side Dishes

# Corn Casserole

This creamy casserole is perfect for company. It's quick and easy and makes a large amount.

> 1 (15-oz.) can whole kernel corn, drained
> 1 (15-oz.) can cream-style corn
> 1 (8.5-oz.) box corn muffin mix
> ¼ cup sugar
> 2 eggs, beaten
> 1 stick butter or margarine, melted
> 1 cup sour cream

Preheat oven to 350°F. Grease a 9-by-13-by-2-inch baking dish.

Children can help stir together corn, muffin mix, sugar, eggs, butter, and sour cream in a large bowl. Pour into baking dish. Bake for 50-60 minutes, or until lightly brown and set.

Serves 8

# Brown and Wild Rice Pilaf

Wild rice costs more than brown or white rice, so it is often mixed with other types of rice. The following recipe captures the pleasing taste that is unique to wild rice.

½ cup wild rice
¼ cup long grain brown rice
3 cups chicken stock
2 tablespoons olive oil
1 medium onion, chopped
1 stalk celery, chopped
1 large carrot, diced
½ teaspoon salt
¼ teaspoon garlic powder
¼ teaspoon Cajun powder
Pepper to taste

Children can help place wild rice in strainer and rinse well under cold running water (wild rice really needs to be well washed); drain. In medium saucepan, combine wild rice, brown rice, and chicken stock. Adult can bring rice mixture to a boil; reduce heat and cover. Simmer for 45 minutes or until tender. Remove from heat.

In skillet, heat olive oil over medium heat. Add onion, celery, and carrots; reduce heat to medium-low and sauté 4-5 minutes until soft. Add this mixture to cooked rice. Children can help measure seasonings. Add to rice mixture. Serve immediately.

Note: This dish can be made ahead of time by placing in greased casserole dish. Refrigerate until 20 minutes before serving time. Reheat in 350°F oven for 20 minutes or in microwave for 5 minutes at high power.

Serves 4

# Desserts

# Cherry-in-the-Middle Cake

This cake is especially good with vanilla ice cream.

4 eggs
1 cup oil
1 cup sugar
2 cups flour
1 teaspoon baking powder
¼ teaspoon salt
1 teaspoon vanilla
2 cans cherry pie filling

## Topping:

¼ cup sugar
1 cup pecans
½ teaspoon cinnamon

Preheat oven to 400°F. Grease and flour a 9-by-12-by-3-inch pan.

Children can help break eggs into a large mixing bowl. Wash hands. Add oil and sugar and mix well with a wooden spoon. Children can help add the flour, baking powder, salt, and vanilla.

**Note: the batter will be sticky and gooey.**

Pour about half the batter into prepared pan. Spread with a spatula. Children can spoon on cherry pie filling, covering up the batter. Pour and spread remaining batter on top of cherries. Mix sugar, pecans, and cinnamon together in a small bowl. Sprinkle on top of batter.

Bake at 400°F for 10 minutes, then turn down to 375°F for 50 minutes.

*Makes 24 pieces*

# Favorite Apple Betty

4 cups cooking apples
⅓ cup sugar
1 teaspoon cinnamon
¾ cup hot water

Combine apples, sugar, cinnamon, and water in a medium-sized pot. Bring to a boil and simmer for 5 – 8 minutes. Pour into an ungreased 9-inch pie pan. Sprinkle with the following crumb topping:

## Crumb Topping

½ cup brown sugar
¼ cup shortening
2 tablespoons butter or margarine
1 cup flour
1 teaspoon baking powder
¼ teaspoon salt

Children can help blend brown sugar, shortening, and butter with a pastry blender. Add remaining ingredients and mix well. Mixture will be crumbly. Sprinkle over apples.

Bake at 350°F for 25-30 minutes. Serve warm or cold.

Serves 6.

# Razzmatazz Raspberry Sauce

1 (12-oz.) package frozen, lightly-
    sweetened, red raspberries, thawed
Water
2 tablespoons sugar
1 tablespoon cornstarch
⅛ teaspoon ground allspice
2 teaspoons vanilla

Sieve the raspberries and discard the seeds. Add water to the raspberry puree to equal 1 ¼ cups. Children can help measure sugar, cornstarch, and allspice; add to puree. Place in saucepan and cook, stirring frequently, over medium heat, until thick and bubbly. Remove from heat. Add vanilla.

Store covered in refrigerator. Serve over fresh fruit, ice cream or angel food cake.

*Makes 1 ¼ cups sauce*

# Oatmeal Goodie Bars

Minnesota is the leading oat-growing state in the United States. Besides eating oats as a breakfast cereal, oats give baked goods a wonderful texture and taste.

1 cup packed brown sugar
1 cup oil
2 eggs
2 cups quick-cooking oatmeal
¾ cup white flour
¾ cup whole wheat flour
1 teaspoon baking soda
¼ teaspoon salt
1 ½ teaspoons cinnamon
1 ½ teaspoons cloves
1 cup raisins
1 cup coconut

Preheat oven to 350°F. Children can grease a jelly roll pan, 15-by-10-by-1-inch or use a 9-by-13-by-2-inch pan.

Children can help measure sugar, oil, and eggs into a large bowl; stir with a wooden spoon until smooth. Add oatmeal, white flour, wheat flour, baking soda, salt, cinnamon, cloves, raisins, and coconut. Mix well. Pour and spread into prepared pan.

Bake about 15 minutes for jelly roll pan, 15-20 minutes for 9-by-13-inch pan, just until center is set. Cool; cut into bars about 3 inches long.

## Makes about 25 bars

## Variation:

Chocolate Chip Goodie bars: substitute 1 cup semisweet chocolate chips for the raisins. Omit the cinnamon and cloves.

# Oatmeal Mix-in-the-Pan Cake

1 ⅔ cups flour
¾ cup oatmeal (quick cooking)
1 cup brown sugar
1 teaspoon baking soda
½ teaspoon salt
1 teaspoon allspice
½ cup raisins
2 tablespoons molasses
1 cup water
⅓ cup oil
1 teaspoon vinegar
½ teaspoon vanilla
Powdered sugar, if desired

Preheat oven to 350°F. No need to grease pan.

Children can help measure dry ingredients and raisins into an 8-by-8-inch square pan. Add molasses to water, stir, then pour into pan. Children can stir in oil, vinegar, and vanilla. Mix until well blended. Smooth batter evenly into corners.

Bake 35-40 minutes, or until a toothpick inserted in center comes out clean. Using a sifter or strainer, shake a layer of powdered sugar on top.

*Serves 9-12*

# Heartland

**Iowa**
**Kansas**
**Missouri**
**Nebraska**
**North Dakota**
**South Dakota**

## Activities:

- Plan a centerpiece. Children can place a colorful tea towel in a basket with a handle. Arrange ears of corn in the basket.
- Make your own peanut butter. George Washington Carver was born in Diamond Grove, Missouri. He was primarily a scientist but is perhaps better known for developing peanut butter. See page 83 to try your hand at making this delicious spread.
- Grow an avocado plant. After making Marla's Corn Salad on page 160, keep the avocado pit. Then fill a drinking glass or jar with water. Poke three toothpicks into the side of the avocado pit and suspend it into the water, balancing the pit on the edge of the glass or jar. Place the pointed side of the pit face up. The rounded side of the pit should be touching the water. Roots should begin to grow in four to six weeks. Then plant the pit in potting soil in a 12-inch pot.
- Read books by Samuel Clemens (the author Mark Twain), who was born in Florida, Missouri. Note to see if he mentions what they ate.

- Grow prairie grasses. Grow grass seed in a paper cup to symbolize the great fields of the heartland. All you need is dirt, seed, water and sun.
- Buy and prepare various kinds of corn for a "corny meal". Buy and compare yellow corn, white (shoepeg) corn, creamed corn, and hominy. Make Sweet and Spicy Beef and Vegetable Stew (see page 158).

## Regional Description

The Heartland is in the "heart" or center of the USA. A large part of the Heartland is flat, but not all of it. The rolling hills of Missouri blend into the peaks of the Ozark Mountains. The large area of plains and prairies produces more corn and wheat than any other region. It is often referred to as the "breadbasket" of the nation.

Iowa leads the nation in producing corn, hogs, pigs, and eggs. It is also one of the top milk producing states. The Heartland states are the second largest producers of cattle. Other major agricultural products include oats, barley, sugar beets, and honey.

Kansas, Nebraska, and the Dakotas grow millions of bushels of wheat each year. A field of wheat blowing in the wind is "the amber waves of grain" in the song, "America the Beautiful." Wheat, ground into flour, is the main ingredient in bread, pasta, baked goods, and breakfast cereal. Notice how you eat wheat at almost every meal and in every snack.

# Breads

# Homemade Cinnamon-Raisin Biscuits

When my daughters were younger, they always enjoyed having a bit of dough they could roll out with their child-sized rolling pin.

2 cups flour
3 teaspoons baking powder
2 tablespoons sugar
1 teaspoon salt
1 teaspoon cinnamon
¼ cup shortening
½ cup raisins
¾ cup milk

Preheat oven to 450°F.

Children can help measure flour, baking powder, sugar, salt and cinnamon into a medium-sized mixing bowl. Cut in shortening with a pastry blender or two knives until mixture has a coarse texture, about the size of small peas. Add raisins and milk, stirring with a fork to make soft dough.

Turn out on a floured board or pastry cloth. Children will have fun pushing or kneading dough with floured hands. Knead 20 times. Roll ½-inch thick with a floured rolling pin. Cut with a 2-inch biscuit cutter or glass. Bake for 10-12 minutes or until lightly browned. Spread icing on hot biscuits before serving.

**Icing:** mix ½ cup powdered sugar, 2 teaspoons milk, and ½ teaspoon vanilla until smooth.

## Makes 10 biscuits

# Quick 'n Easy Cinnamon Biscuits

1 tablespoon sugar
½ teaspoon cinnamon
1 (7-oz.) can biscuits

Preheat oven according to package directions. Children can mix sugar and cinnamon in a cereal bowl. Dip tops of biscuits in cinnamon mixture. Place, cinnamon-side up, on an ungreased baking sheet. Bake according to package directions. Serve with butter.

## Makes 10 biscuits

# Sunflower Seed Bread

We drove along the flat land and straight roads of Kansas, until we saw what my father-in-law, Lyle, brought us to see: acres of full-grown sunflowers, yellow blooms facing upward, packed with seeds, ready for harvest. What a sight! Did you know they always face the sun?

Sunflower seeds are a fun snack, or topping for salad. Here is a unique bread made with sunflower seeds, which give it a rich, taste and crunchy texture. This bread is easily made in a bread machine.

1 cup plus 3 tablespoons water
3 tablespoons honey
1 teaspoon salt
½ cup old-fashioned oats
2 cups bread flour
1 cup whole wheat flour
1 tablespoon yeast
⅓ cup hulled sunflower seeds

Children can help measure and place ingredients, EXCEPT sunflower seeds, into bread machine pan. Follow manufacturer's directions, using the "wheat" setting, if possible.

Add sunflower seeds just before the last kneading, or they will be ground much too fine.

*Makes 1 – 1 ½ pound loaf*

# Elephant French Toast

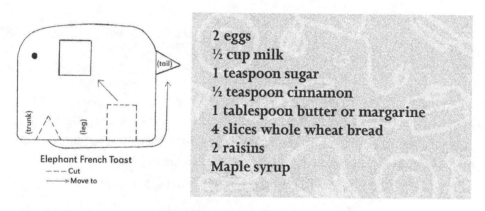

Elephant French Toast
- - - Cut
⟶ Move to

**2 eggs**
**½ cup milk**
**1 teaspoon sugar**
**½ teaspoon cinnamon**
**1 tablespoon butter or margarine**
**4 slices whole wheat bread**
**2 raisins**
**Maple syrup**

Beat eggs in a medium-sized mixing bowl. Children can help measure and add milk, sugar, and cinnamon to eggs; beat with a wire whisk or fork. Melt butter in a large skillet over medium heat. Dip bread into egg mixture and carefully place in skillet. Fry a few minutes on each side, until golden brown. Remove to a serving plate.

For each elephant: use one piece of bread. Cut out a square for the ear and a triangle for the tail. Place raisin in front of ear for eye. Pour on maple syrup.

*Makes 4 elephants*

# Super Snack Mix

3 cups square rice cereal
3 cups square corn cereal
3 cups square wheat cereal
1 cup pretzels
1 cup bagel chips
1 cup mixed nuts
6 tablespoons butter or margarine, melted
¾ teaspoon garlic powder
½ teaspoon onion powder
1 ½ teaspoons seasoned salt
2 tablespoons Worcestershire sauce

Preheat oven to 250°F.

Children can help measure and mix ingredients. Measure and pour cereal, pretzels, bagel chips, and nuts into a large roasting pan. Stir seasonings into melted butter. Drizzle butter mixture over cereal mixture; stir with a large wooden spoon to coat cereal.

Bake 1 hour, stirring every 15 minutes. Spread on paper towels to cool. Store in an airtight container.

*Makes 12 cups*

# Soups, Salads, and Sandwiches

# Corn

Fields of corn grace the Heartland. Drive in the countryside in Iowa in July, the state that produces the most corn, and you will see row after row, acres and acres of corn, standing tall, crowned with tassels. Besides just good eating, corn is used in other foods. Corn syrup and corn starch are used in ice cream, chewing gum, cookies, and ketchup. Cows, pigs, and chickens eat corn, but they eat "feed corn," instead of "sweet corn" that people eat. Feed corn is tough, dry, and not sweet-tasting like the corn we eat.

# Sweet and Spicy Beef and Vegetable Stew

1 sweet red pepper, diced
1 pound ground beef
1 onion, diced
1 (16-oz.) bag frozen corn or 2 cups fresh corn niblets, cut off the cob
1 (46-oz.) can tomato or vegetable juice
Salt and pepper to taste
Dash cinnamon

After you prepare the red pepper by rinsing, removing the seeds and dicing, children can taste a little bit of it. An adult can brown ground beef, pepper, and onion in a skillet until beef is cooked and browned and the vegetables are tender. Remove beef and vegetables with a slotted spoon to a 4-quart pot to drain grease. Discard grease.

Children can help add corn and tomato juice to pot. Heat over high heat to boiling, then turn down heat to low and simmer about 20 minutes, until corn is cooked. Add salt and pepper to taste. Add a dash of cinnamon just before serving.

Serves 6–8

# Steak Soup
*This soup has a delicious flavor.*

2 cups cooked beef roast or 1 ½ pounds
   ground beef
2 cups diced onions
1 cup diced carrots
1 cup diced celery
1 tablespoon minced garlic
5 cups water and 5 bouillon cubes
1 (16-oz.) can crushed tomatoes, with
     juice
2 tablespoons Worcestershire sauce
1 teaspoon red pepper sauce
½ teaspoon freshly ground pepper
¼ cup butter or margarine
½ cup flour

If using cooked beef roast, cut into small pieces. If using ground beef, brown in a large skillet over medium heat.

Dice vegetables while meat cooks. Allow children to sniff onions, nibble on a carrot or celery stick. When ground beef is browned, drain grease. Add vegetables to skillet and cook about 10 minutes until softened.

Children can help measure water and bouillon cubes into a large pot. Add beef mixture, tomatoes, Worcestershire sauce, pepper sauce, and ground pepper. Bring to a boil over high heat; turn down to low, cover and simmer 15 minutes.

Meanwhile, melt butter in a small saucepan over medium heat. Children can measure flour. Add to saucepan, stirring constantly, until flour has browned. Stir this into the soup with a wire whisk; cover and simmer an additional 15 minutes.

# Marla's Corn Salad

1 (11-oz.) can corn with red and
  green peppers, drained
1 (15-oz.) can black beans, with
  liquid
1 bunch scallions
½ cup oil
2 tablespoons red wine vinegar
4 small tomatoes
2 avocados
Salt and pepper to taste

An adult can chop scallions. Children can help measure, add, and mix ingredients. Pour corn and beans into a bowl. Add scallions, oil, and vinegar; stir. Refrigerate.

Just before serving, dice and add tomatoes. Peel, pit, and dice avocados. Add to salad. Season to taste with salt and pepper. Serve.

Serves 6–8

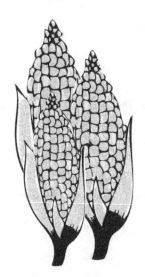

# Popcorn, a Special Type of Corn

Not all corn can be popped. Popcorn comes from a special type of corn. If you tried popping other types of corn kernels, they would not pop, but popcorn kernels do. Americans eat a lot of popcorn! According to the Popcorn Board, "Americans today consume 17 billion quarts of popped popcorn each year. The average American eats about 58 quarts."

# Popcorn "Experiment"

Did you know that science and cooking go together? Cooking is based on scientific principles and chemical reactions. Cooking allows you to use all of your senses to make discoveries and comparisons. You can see, taste, touch, smell, and even hear food. The popping sound of popcorn as the kernel bursting open from the heat is an example of the sound of food. Try this popcorn experiment.

2 tablespoons butter, if desired
¼ cup oil
⅓ cup popcorn kernels
Salt to taste

**Procedure:** Melt butter in microwave and reserve. Children can measure oil and place in a large (4 quart) pot. Add one or 2 popcorn kernels. Adult can place pot over medium-high heat.

What do you think will happen when heat is applied to popcorn kernels? Discuss your prediction.

When kernels pop, add the remaining popcorn kernels to pot and cover. Shake pot to prevent burning. Listen! When popcorn noise slows, remove from heat. Turn out into a big bowl. Children can shake on salt and add melted butter, if desired.

Compare the unpopped kernels to the popped corn. How are they alike or different? Did you like the popping noise? Of what did it remind you?

Now you have seen, smelled, heard, and touched the popcorn. Now taste it!

**Conclusion:** Was your prediction correct? Did you predict that the kernels would pop when heat was applied to them? Good job!

Note: Young children 4 years and younger can choke on popcorn.

# B.L.T. Sandwiches (Bacon, Lettuce and Tomato)

When I pick a tomato off the vine from my garden, I immediately think of making a B.L.T. There is nothing quite like this taste. The juicy tomato, salty bacon, and crisp lettuce make a perfect combination! For a healthier sandwich, use turkey bacon, which is lower in fat.

8 slices bacon
2 tomatoes
4 onion slices, optional
4 lettuce leaves
8 slices whole wheat bread
2 tablespoons mayonnaise
Salt and pepper

Adult can fry bacon over medium-low heat until crisp; drain on paper towels. Adult can core and slice tomato into ¼-inch rounds and slice onion. Children can rinse lettuce leaves and pat dry with paper towel. Toast bread. Spread with mayonnaise.

Assemble sandwiches with 2 slices bacon, 1-2 slices tomato, onion as desired, and 1 lettuce leaf. Sprinkle tomato with salt and pepper, if desired. Cut in half for easy handling, or cut in fourths and insert toothpick in each quarter.

Variation:
B.L.T. Club Sandwich: Use 3 slices of toast and additional filling for a triple-decker sandwich.

Makes 4 sandwiches

# Main Dishes/ Meats

The Heartland states are noted for their choice meat selections of beef and pork. Many beef steaks, roasts, and other cuts of meat are featured in restaurants and back-yard picnics.

# All-American Hamburgers

Large herds of beef cattle graze on the prairie grasses of the Heartland. Hamburgers are one of the most popular American foods. The average American eats 3 burgers per week. Some of the highest quality beef comes from the Midwest. Which burger topping is your favorite?

**1 pound lean ground beef**
**Salt and pepper to taste**
**4 hamburger buns**

Make sure children wash hands well before and after handling raw meat.

Children can help to form beef patties, 4 patties per pound.

Grill, broil or fry on medium-high heat to sear in flavor, flip over, then turn down heat and cook until done, about 10-20 minutes total, depending on the thickness of the burger. Remove from heat. Children can sprinkle with salt and pepper. Toast buns.

Favorite toppings: ketchup, mustard, dill pickles, thinly sliced red onion, American cheese, bacon strips, mayonnaise, lettuce, tomato.

# Kansas City Barbecue

Kansas City is famous for barbecue. The sweet and sour sauce is a perfect complement to beef or pork - a great way to use yesterday's roast.

Beef or pork roast, sliced thinly
or shredded
Barbecue sauce (see recipe following)
Hamburger buns

Place meat in a saucepan. Children can help pour sauce over meat, mixing gently with a fork. Heat meat and barbecue sauce, covered, over low heat until heated though. Serve on toasted buns.

# Barbecue Sauce

1 cup ketchup
2 tablespoons cider vinegar
1 tablespoon Worcestershire sauce
1 teaspoon sugar
Salt and pepper to taste

Children can help measure ingredients into a small saucepan; stir. Adult can heat mixture over medium-high heat just until it comes to a boil.

*Makes about 1 1/4 cups*

# Sausage, Peppers, and ✪nions

Pork is meat that comes from hogs and pigs. Young animals are called pigs and older ones are hogs. Several delicious pork foods are: ham, bacon, pork chops, and sausage. Pork sausage is a mixture of ground pork, pork fat, and spices.

> **1 pound link pork sausage, mild
>      or hot**
> **1 green pepper, cut in strips**
> **½ large onion, sliced**
> **1 tablespoon butter**

Children can prepare green pepper by washing, cutting out core, halving, and taking out the seeds. Cut into strips. Slice onion. Adult can melt butter in skillet and add pepper and onions, cooking until vegetables are tender and soft. Remove to serving platter, cover, and keep warm.

Brown pork sausage links in same skillet. Prick sausages in a few places to release excess fat. Turn frequently to brown evenly. To tell whether sausages are done, cut one in half. If there is no pink showing, the sausages are cooked. Drain on paper towel and serve with the vegetables.

*Serves 4*

# Vegetables / Side Dishes

# Velma's Cole Slaw and Dressing

*A perfect accompaniment for your favorite burger.*

⅓ cup mayonnaise
1 tablespoon cider vinegar
3 tablespoons sugar
½ teaspoon celery seed
3 cups shredded cabbage
1 carrot, grated

Children can help measure and mix mayonnaise, vinegar, sugar, and celery seed in a small bowl. Toss with cabbage and carrot.

*Serves 4*

# Green Beans with Bacon

*Bacon makes these beans taste great!*

2 cups fresh green beans
2 slices bacon
1 small onion, chopped

Rinse green beans. Children can help break off ends and snap in half. In a skillet over medium-low heat, fry bacon until crisp. Remove bacon from skillet. Fry onion in bacon grease about 5 minutes or until tender. Meanwhile, in a medium-sized pot, bring 1 inch water to boil. Add green beans; bring back to boil. Turn down heat to low and simmer uncovered for 5 minutes. Then cover and continue to simmer 5 additional minutes. Drain. Pour green beans into a serving dish, mix in onion and top with crumbled bacon.

*Serves 4*

# Desserts

# Chunky Applesauce

While the Heartland is not the top producer of apples, there are many apple trees in the Midwest. This easy recipe cooks apples in the microwave.

> 3 cups pared, cored, sliced baking apples, such as Jonathan or Granny Smith
> ¼ cup sugar
> ¼ cup water

An adult can pare and core apples. Children can help cut into slices using a butter knife. Place in 1½ quart casserole dish. Stir in sugar and water. Cover and microwave on high power for 3 minutes. Stir. Microwave an additional 3 to 6 minutes, stirring once more, until apples are very soft. Let stand covered for 5 minutes. Mash with a potato masher before serving.

# Ice Cream Cone Clown

In 1896, a New York City street vendor, Italo Marchiony, created the ice cream cone and had it patented. The 1904 World's Fair in St. Louis popularized ice cream cones, (as well as hot dogs and iced tea). This dessert for a children's party uses the pointy sugar cone as a hat for a happy clown.

> ½ gallon any flavor ice cream
> Sugar cones
> Raisins
> Dried cranberries

Scoop one ice cream ball per child onto a cookie sheet, cover with plastic wrap and refreeze. Serve each child an ice cream ball. Children can top with cone hat and decorate their own clown faces with raisins for eyes and cranberries for nose and mouth. Keep in mind that the ice cream melts quickly.

# Southwest

**Arizona**
**New Mexico**
**Oklahoma**
**Texas**

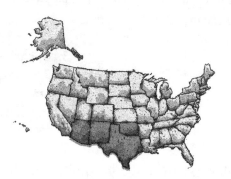

## Activities:

- Create a centerpiece. Children can place nuts in the shell, such as pecans and peanuts, in a clay bowl.
- Celebrate big Texas. When eating a typical Texas meal, such as barbecued ribs, wear your parents' big clothes, serve dinner on platters instead of plates, and eat with big serving forks and spoons.
- Conduct a before and after experiment. Cook burritos (see page 185). Taste the cooked meat before adding the seasoning. Then taste it after you have added seasoning. Which taste do you prefer?
- Fashion a faux (fake) leather vest from a paper grocery sack. Cut a slit up the front, cut out armholes and add "fringes." Wear your "leather" vest to a "Tex-Mex" supper.
- Make a salad using both lettuce and spinach. The southwest grows both types of greens. When washing the spinach, swish and then lift leaves from the water, allowing the dirt to fall to the bottom.
- Plan a cowboy/cowgirl cookout. Have an outdoor barbecue with grilled beef or lamb. Wear your cowboy/cowgirl clothes: big hat, boots, and red bandana.

# Regional Description

As the land spreads out to the west, the Rocky Mountains become the great Continental Divide, or what divides the continent of North America in half. The Southwest is a land of contrasts: the Rocky Mountains give way to dry deserts, grassy plains, and vast prairies.

Because there is little rainfall, resulting in less water, cattle roam on large ranches in search of grass. Beef cattle, sheep, lambs, and turkeys are raised extensively in this area. Texas is ranked #1 for livestock and livestock products. The area also produces corn for grain, wheat, rye, and dairy products.

Arizona produces a good variety of fruit and vegetables, such as oranges, melon, broccoli, cauliflower, lettuce, and spinach. Texas, on the Gulf of Mexico, produces a variety of foods: shrimp, grapefruit, pecans, cabbage, spinach, melon, and more.

There are some wonderful dishes that combine the flavors of Texas and Mexico, which are sometimes labeled "Tex-Mex." Characteristic of these dishes are chili powder, chilies, corn or flour tortillas, and cheese. The flavor is mouthwatering; the dishes are filling, and can satisfy the hungriest members of your family.

# Beverages

# Citrus Sparkle

½ cup grapefruit juice
½ cup orange juice
¼ cup cranberry juice
½ cup club soda
2 lemon wedges

Children can help measure and mix juices and soda in a 1-quart pitcher. Place ice in 2 tall glasses. Pour over ice. Children can squeeze the juice from a lemon wedge into their glass.

## Makes 1 ³/₄ cups

# Cinnamon Tea

Try this spicy tea as an alternative to the traditional cold weather drink, hot cocoa.

5 cups water
4 cinnamon sticks
4 teaspoons sugar

Children can measure water and pour into medium-sized pan. Adult can bring water to boil over high heat. Show children cinnamon sticks and compare to ground cinnamon: see, smell, touch. Children can count out 4 cinnamon sticks. Adult can add to boiling water. Turn down heat and simmer 15 minutes. Remove cinnamon sticks and discard. Add sugar, stir and pour into mugs. Let cool a few minutes before serving.

## Serves 4

# Sugar-Free Lemonade

3 cups water
2 tablespoons lemon juice
¼ cup white grape juice

Children can measure and combine water and juices in a pitcher. Stir. Serve over ice.

This is a refreshing alternative to sugary lemonade.

Serves 6 (one-half-cup servings)

# Appetizers

# Six-Layer Bean Dip

1 package taco seasoning
2 tablespoon water
1 (16-oz.) can refried beans
2 cups guacamole dip (see next recipe)
1 onion, chopped
1 (4-oz.) can chopped green chilies
1 (2.25-oz.) can sliced black olives
2 cups grated Monterey-Jack cheese
1 (16-oz) bag tortilla chips

Children can help mix taco seasoning and water in a medium-sized bowl; add refried beans, stirring to combine. Spread in a glass 9-by-13-by-2-inch pan. Children can help spread guacamole dip on top of bean dip and sprinkle with onion, chilies, olives, and cheese. Refrigerate until ready to serve. Serve with tortilla chips.

### Makes about 10 servings

# Creamy Guacamole Dip

2-4 ripe avocados
2 tablespoons fresh lemon juice
1 onion, finely chopped
1 tomato, finely chopped
2 tablespoons bottled salsa
Salt and cayenne pepper to taste

Children can help peel avocados, remove pit and mash. Add lemon juice, onion, tomato, salsa, and salt and pepper to taste. Serve with chips.

# Breads

# Confetti Corn Bread

Red and green chilies look like confetti in this cheesy cornbread.

1 ¼ cups flour
¾ cup yellow corn meal
¼ cup sugar
2 teaspoons baking powder
½ teaspoon salt
1 cup milk
1 (8 ½-oz.) can creamed corn
1 (4-oz.) can diced mild green chilies
    and/or diced pimentos
¼ cup oil
1 egg, beaten
½ cup grated sharp Cheddar cheese

Preheat oven to 400°F. Grease a 9-inch square pan.

Children can measure flour, cornmeal, sugar, baking powder, and salt into a medium-sized bowl. Make a well in the center and add milk, corn, chilies, oil, egg, and cheese. Mix just until dry ingredients are moistened, about 50 strokes.

Pour into prepared pan. Bake 20 – 25 minutes or until light brown. Cut into 9 squares. Best served warm with plenty of butter.

## Easy variation:

Use 2 packages corn bread mix, made according to package directions, adding 1 (8 ½-oz.) can creamed corn, 1 (4-oz.) can diced mild green chilies, and ½ cup grated sharp Cheddar cheese.

Makes 9 servings

# Cheese 'n Pepper Quesadillas

Serve this scrumptious dish as an appetizer, snack or light meal.

8 flour tortillas
Butter or margarine, softened
1 cup grated Cheddar cheese
1 (4-oz.) can chopped mild green chilies

This is made like a grilled cheese sandwich using tortillas instead of bread. Children can help spread butter on a flour tortilla. Turn over and place on a plate buttered-side down. Sprinkle with ¼ cup grated cheese and a teaspoon or so of chilies. Spread butter on a second tortilla. Turn buttered-side up; place on top of cheese mixture.

An adult can transfer cheese-filled tortilla to a skillet, which has been heated on medium. Cover; fry for a few minutes until browned. Carefully turn over, cover and fry on remaining side. Remove from skillet and keep warm in oven. Repeat with remaining ingredients to made 4 quesadillas. To serve, cut into eighths.

Makes 4 servings

# Salads

## Citrus Salad

> 1 grapefruit
> 1 orange
> 2 tablespoons orange juice
> 2 maraschino cherries
> 2 mint leaves

Children can help peel grapefruit and orange, discarding peel as well as the white membrane which is bitter tasting. Divide fruit into sections and place in a medium-sized bowl. Add orange juice and stir. Spoon into serving bowls. Cut cherries in half. Place a cherry half and sprig of mint on top. Serve.

### Makes 4 servings

# Main Dishes / Meats

# Tamale Pie

Beef is a favorite in the Southwest and readily available. This savory meat pie has a cornbread crust.

1 pound lean ground beef
1 onion, chopped
1 large green pepper, chopped
1 (15-oz.) can tomato sauce
1 (16-oz.) can corn
½ teaspoon salt
2 teaspoons chili powder
1 cup grated Cheddar cheese

## Crust:

⅔ cups flour
⅓ cup yellow corn meal
2 tablespoons sugar
1 teaspoon baking powder
¼ teaspoon salt
½ cup milk
2 tablespoons oil
1 egg, beaten
½ cup grated Cheddar cheese

Preheat oven to 375°F.

Adult can brown ground beef, onions, and green pepper in a large skillet over medium heat; drain grease. Add tomato sauce, corn, salt, and chili powder. Heat to boiling; reduce heat to low and simmer, uncovered, for 5 minutes. Stir in cheese. Pour into a 2-quart casserole dish.

Prepare crust. Children can measure flour, cornmeal, sugar, baking powder, and salt into a medium-sized bowl. Make a well in the center and add milk, oil, and egg. Mix just until dry ingredients are moistened, about 50 strokes. Pour over meat mixture in casserole.

Bake for about 40 to 45 minutes or until crust is cooked through. Sprinkle with ½ cup grated cheese over the crust about 5 minutes before casserole is done.

## Easy variation:
Substitute an 8.5-oz. box of cornbread mix for the crust. Mix according to package directions.

*Serves 6*

# Beef Burritos

1 pound ground beef
1 teaspoon chili powder
¼ teaspoon cumin
⅛ teaspoon oregano
1 tablespoon corn starch
½ cup beef broth or bouillon
Bottled picante sauce
1 package flour tortillas
1 cup grated Monterey Jack cheese

Adult can brown ground beef in skillet over medium heat until no pink is left; drain grease. Children can help measure chili powder, cumin, oregano, and cornstarch into a bowl. Add spice mixture to skillet; stir. Add broth and a spoonful of picante sauce, stirring until thickened. Turn down heat to low and let simmer a few minutes. Add broth or water if the mixture gets too thick.

Heat flour tortillas in microwave or regular oven according to package directions. To serve, spoon beef onto warm tortilla, sprinkle with cheese and a spoonful of Picante sauce. Fold about a third of tortilla up, then roll up tortilla from left to right to form a cylinder. Serve immediately.

*Makes about 6 to 8 burritos*

# Cowboy Chili

1 pound ground beef
1 onion, chopped
1 green pepper, diced
2 teaspoons chili powder
1 (16-oz.) can diced tomatoes
1 (8-oz.) can tomato sauce
½ teaspoon salt
1 (15 ½-oz.) can kidney beans
1 cup grated Cheddar cheese

Adult can brown ground beef, onion, and pepper in skillet over medium heat; drain grease. Children can help to measure spices. Add chili powder, salt, tomatoes, and tomato sauce. Cover and simmer for 1 to 2 hours on low heat.

Five minutes before serving, pour beans into a colander. Children can help rinse beans under cold water. Add to pot. Pass Cheddar cheese at the table. Serve with crackers and tortilla chips.

*Makes 4 servings*

# Cowgirl Grill

This is a mighty fine meal for hungry cowboys and cowgirls who have been riding the range all day.

1 pound ground beef
4 potatoes, pared and sliced
4 carrots, pared and sliced
Salt and pepper to taste

An adult can light coals on barbecue grill. Use heavy duty tin foil. Children can help place potato slices, hamburger patty, and carrot slices on foil. Sprinkle with salt and pepper. Fold foil to completely encase meat and vegetable mixture.

Place down in coals for 15 minutes; turn and cook an additional 15 minutes, or until meat and vegetables are cooked. Eat outside with fork on foil "plate." Serve with "Texas Toast," which is double-thick sliced white bread.

Serves 4

# Beef Jerky

Pioneers and cowboys would bring dried beef, such as this, on their travels as it doesn't need to be refrigerated.

2 pounds flank steak
½ cup soy sauce
Garlic salt
Lemon pepper

Preheat oven to 150°F.

Place steak in freezer about 15 minutes to make slicing easier. Adult should slice beef thinly, across (against) the grain; place in a large bowl. Children can help measure soy sauce and pour over meat; stir to coat. Drain sauce.

Place strips of steak in a single layer on an ungreased cookie sheet. Sprinkle with garlic salt and lemon pepper. Bake 10 hours. Cool. Store in an airtight container.

*Makes about ¹/₂ pound*

# Barbecued Ribs

**5 pounds beef short ribs**
**Bottled barbecue sauce**

Place ribs in a large (8-quart) pot. Children can help cover ribs with water. Adult can bring water and ribs to boiling over high heat. Cover, turn down to low and simmer for 2 hours, until ribs are cooked and tender. Remove from pot and either grill or broil 20-25 minutes, brushing with barbecue sauce and turning often.

*Serves 4-6*

# Boiled Shrimp

Gulf Coast foods include seafood and fish. This is a big business in Texas.

**2 pounds fresh shrimp**
**1 teaspoon salt**

Children can help peel shrimp. Peel back shell, hold onto tail and gently pull. Carefully remove the vein with a toothpick or under running water.

Heat 2-quarts of water and salt to boiling in a large pot over high heat. Add shrimp. Bring to second boil, turn down heat simmer for 1 to 3 minutes (depending on size of shrimp) until it turns pink. Drain. Serve hot with Creole Sauce, page 115, or serve cold with Cocktail Sauce, page 90.

Serves 4

# Shrimp and Pasta

1 pound medium shrimp
1 (8-oz.) package pasta, such as wide egg noodles, linguini or angel hair pasta
4 tablespoons olive oil
2 cloves of garlic, minced
2 teaspoons lemon pepper
½ cup grated Parmesan cheese

Children can help peel shrimp. Peel back shell, hold onto tail and gently pull. Carefully remove the vein with a toothpick or under running water.

Adult can boil pasta according to package directions; drain.

Heat oil in a large skillet over medium heat. Add garlic, shrimp, and lemon pepper seasoning and sauté for a few minutes, until shrimp turns pink. Add pasta and Parmesan cheese; stir and serve.

Serves 4

# Side Dishes

## Spanish Rice

1 small onion, chopped fine
1 green pepper, chopped fine
¼ cup olive oil
1 cup rice
1 (14.5-oz.) can chopped tomatoes
1 cup water
1 teaspoon salt
1 tablespoon chili powder
1 tablespoon fresh, or 1 teaspoon dried, chopped parsley

Sauté onion and pepper in oil in a 2-quart saucepan over medium heat for a few minutes. Add rice, stirring constantly, until rice becomes a very light brown. Remove from heat and add the tomatoes.

Children can help measure water, salt, and chili powder. Add this mixture to the saucepan and place back over the heat. Bring to a boil over high heat. Turn down heat to very low, cover, and simmer without lifting the cover for about 25 minutes, or until the water is absorbed. Let stand 5 minutes. Add parsley and serve.

*Makes 4 servings*

# Desserts

# Texas Sheet Cake

One big difference in this cake is you frost it while it's hot. The chocolate, nut-studded icing turns into a candy-like glaze. This recipe can be mixed by hand— no electric mixer required!

2 cups sugar
2 cups flour
¼ cup cocoa
1 teaspoon baking soda
1 teaspoon cinnamon
½ cup (1 stick) butter or margarine,
    melted
½ cup buttermilk or sour milk (for sour
    milk, mix ½ scant cup milk and
    ½ tablespoon vinegar and let set 5
    minutes)
½ cup oil
1 cup water
2 eggs, lightly beaten
1 teaspoon vanilla

Preheat oven to 400°F. Grease and flour a 13-by-9-by-2-inch baking pan.

Children can help measure sugar, flour, cocoa, baking soda, and cinnamon into a large bowl; stir. Make a well in the center. Add butter, buttermilk, oil, water, eggs, and vanilla. Batter will be thin.

Pour into prepared pan, and bake for 30-35 minutes, or until a toothpick comes out clean. Prepare the frosting (see next page) while the cake is baking, and frost hot cake when it comes out of oven.

# Cocoa-Pecan Frosting

¼ cup plus 2 tablespoons milk
¼ cup cocoa
½ cup (1 stick) butter or margarine
1 (16-oz.) package powdered sugar, sifted
1 teaspoon vanilla
1 cup chopped pecans

Children can help measure and mix the milk and cocoa in a large
(4-quart) heavy saucepan. Add butter. Adult can place over medium heat
and stir until butter melts. Remove from heat and add the sugar and
vanilla; stir until smooth. Mix in the pecans. Spread the frosting over the
hot cake when it comes out of the oven.

Serves 24

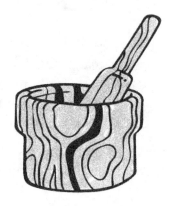

# Bread Pudding

2 ½ cups milk
⅓ cup raisins (optional)
4 slices bread
2 tablespoons butter or margarine
⅓ cup packed brown sugar
½ teaspoon cinnamon
3 eggs
⅓ cup white sugar
1 teaspoon vanilla
⅛ teaspoon salt

Preheat oven to 350°F. Children can butter a 1½-quart casserole dish. Sprinkle raisins in dish.

Fill a 9x13x2-inch pan with approximately an inch of water and place in oven while preheating to heat water. Scald milk by heating to almost boiling; remove from heat and set aside.

Toast bread on light setting. Children can spread toast with butter. Sprinkle 2 slices of bread with brown sugar and cinnamon. Place 2 remaining slices of bread on top, like a sandwich. Cut into fourths. Place in casserole dish on top of raisins, in a single layer.

Children can help beat eggs in a medium-sized bowl. Stir in white sugar, vanilla, and salt.

Adult can gradually add scalded milk. Pour over bread. Place casserole dish in pan of water in oven. Bake about 65 minutes or until pudding is set. Remove casserole dish from water. Serve warm or cold. Store in refrigerator.

Serves 6-8

# Cinnamon Crisps

Oil
**4 flour tortillas**
**¼ cup sugar**
**½ teaspoon cinnamon**

Heat oil in a deep fat fryer to 370°F. or about ½ inch oil in a skillet over medium heat. Children can cut flour tortillas into eighths using a butter knife and a cutting board. Mix sugar and cinnamon in a small bowl.

Adult can fry tortillas in oil just a few seconds, until crisp. Remove from pan and drain on paper towel lined plate. Children can sprinkle with cinnamon mixture. Eat as a snack or dessert.

Serves 4

# Mountain States

**Colorado**
**Idaho**
**Montana**
**Nevada**
**Utah**
**Wyoming**

## Activities:

- Create a centerpiece. Children can make "potato head" people by using raisin eyes, cherry tomato half noses, and green pepper slices for mouths. Adult can help secure features using a straight pin.
- Count the many types of potatoes on the market. Idaho is famous for the potatoes it produces. Next time you are at the grocery store, count the types of frozen potatoes they sell, such as, hash browns, French fries, etc.
- Make garlic bread. Garlic is one of the products of the Mountain States. Make garlic bread by mincing garlic, mixing it with butter, spreading it on bread and toasting or heating it until the bread is warm and the butter is melted.
- Plan a fun snow day on the day school is closed. What will you do? Will you bake bread or cookies, and then play in the snow? What would you eat?

- Catch falling snow in a paper cup. Drizzle maple syrup over top for a yummy treat.
- Use honey in place of sugar in one of your favorite recipes. For this, reduce the amount of liquid by ¼ cup for each cup of honey. For example, if your recipe lists 1 cup milk and 1 cup sugar, substitute ¾ cup milk and 1 cup honey.
- Research the history of sour dough bread. How did it help the pioneers with their food preparation? What makes sour dough bread rise?

## Regional Description

The Mountain States, also referred to as Mountain West, are a region of vast contrasts. These range from snow covered mountain peaks with their varying rock formations to bubbling hot springs and wide open prairies. The word "Mountain" refers to the Rocky Mountains, which run north-south throughout the division.

This region leads in producing potatoes and is a top producer of sheep, barley, wheat, garlic, spinach, sugar beets, and honey. The climate is very dry and irrigation is used to provide enough moisture for growing crops. Cattle and sheep graze in the vast ranges of the Mountain States in order to find enough grass to eat.

The area is deeply rooted in the exploration and settlement of North America. The Lewis and Clark route, as well as the Oregon Trail, cuts through this region. It was the scene of great activity during the gold rush days. Attending rodeos is now a popular pastime.

# Breads

# Sourdough Starter

Sourdough bread has been in existence for thousands of years. It was a popular method of making bread when the pioneers traveled westward in covered wagons. Since yeast as we know it today was not available, they used a wild yeast formed from a "starter" to make their bread rise. The starter is a bubbly batter made basically of flour and water in which wild yeast can grow. People continue to make and use sourdough starters because they enjoy the distinctive tangy taste of this type of bread. Here is a modernized starter using dry yeast to jump-start the bubbling action of the batter.

> 1 (¼-oz.) package or 2½ teaspoons
>    active dry yeast
> 2 cups warm water *
> 2 cups flour

Children can help measure and mix the ingredients.

Dissolve yeast in water* in a ceramic or glass bowl (not metal) by mixing with a wooden spoon.

*\* Note: use warm, not hot water, or you will kill the yeast. A good way to test the temperature of the water is to sprinkle a few drops on your wrist, like testing a baby bottle. If it feels warm, not hot or cool to your wrist, it is the right temperature for the yeast.*

Add flour and stir until blended. The batter will be thin and lumpy.

Set the bowl on the kitchen counter, in a warm place, such as near the range. Leave uncovered, 48 hours, stirring occasionally. Now the starter is ready to use in the following recipes. You and your children can observe the changes in the yeast mixture: notice how the size, color, and pungent smell changes.

## Replenishing the Starter

When you use a part of the starter in a recipe, add equal parts of flour and warm water to the remaining starter to keep it going. This is called "replenishing" the starter. Some people have had their starter going for years! Once you replenish your starter, let it set on the counter for about 8 hours, or until it bubbles. Then cover loosely, and store in refrigerator.

To keep your starter going, use it at least once every other week. Children can help you replenish your starter once you use it. If you don't want to keep the starter going, use all of it in a recipe(s).

# Sour Dough Bread

¼ cup water
1 tablespoon sugar
1 cup Sourdough Starter (see page 200)
1 teaspoon salt
2 ¼ cups bread flour
1 teaspoon active-dry yeast

Children can help measure ingredients into bread machine in order listed. Follow manufacturer's directions for white bread. Let cool before slicing if you can wait!

## Makes 1 loaf

# Sour Dough Pancakes

2 cups starter (see page 200)
2 eggs, beaten
2 teaspoons baking powder
1 teaspoon baking soda
1 teaspoon salt
2 tablespoons sugar
¼ cup oil
Butter
Maple syrup

If starter is in refrigerator, measure 2 cups into bowl (not metal) and cover. Leave at room temperature. (This can be done a day or two before making pancakes.) Replenish original batch, if desired, and refrigerate.

Children can help beat eggs in a large bowl. Add starter, baking powder, baking soda, salt, sugar, and oil. An adult should heat the griddle to 400°F. Grease with oil. Ladle batter onto griddle to make large pancakes. When edges start to brown, turn and cook on other side. Serve with plenty of butter and maple syrup.

## Variation:

Silver Dollar Pancakes: use recipe above, only make pancakes smaller, such as the old-fashioned silver dollar size. Stack high when serving.

*Makes about 16 pancakes*

# Soups, Salads, and Sandwiches

# Beef-Barley Soup

The Mountain States grow barley, a wonderful addition to vegetable soup.

1 pound lean ground beef
1 onion, chopped
1 carrot, diced
2 ribs celery, diced
6 cups water
1 cup medium barley
1 (16-oz.) chopped tomatoes, with juice
1 teaspoon dried parsley
2 teaspoons salt
¼ teaspoon pepper

In a large (4-quart) pot, cook ground beef over medium heat; drain grease. Add onion, carrot, and celery. Cook, stirring occasionally, for about 5 minutes.

Children can measure water and barley, parsley, salt, and pepper. Adult can add water, barley, tomatoes, parsley, salt, and pepper to pot. Bring to a boil over high heat. Turn down heat to low, cover and simmer about an hour.

Serves 6–8

# Wilted Spinach Salad

*This salad has a delightful sweet and sour flavor.*

10 oz. fresh spinach leaves
4 slices bacon, diced
¼ cup cider vinegar
1 tablespoon sugar
3 scallions, minced
Salt and pepper

Children can rinse spinach by placing it in a big mixing bowl of water and swishing it around to allow the dirt to fall to the bottom. Lift spinach from the water and use a salad spinner or tea towel to remove extra moisture. Remove thick stem from spinach leaves by cutting, pinching, or pulling off. Then place leaves in a large salad bowl.

An adult can cook bacon over medium-low heat until crisp in a large skillet. Add vinegar, sugar, and scallions. Simmer a few minutes, until scallions are tender. Pour dressing over prepared spinach.

Sprinkle with salt and pepper. Toss and serve.

Serves 6-8

# French Dip for Roast Beef Sandwiches

This recipe makes a wonderful broth for dipping roast beef sandwiches.

3 pounds beef chuck or arm roast
2 cups water
½ cup soy sauce
½ teaspoon rosemary
½ teaspoon thyme
½ teaspoon garlic powder
1 bay leaf
Dash pepper
12 hard rolls

Place roast in a crock pot. Children can help measure and add water, soy sauce, and spices to crock pot. Cook 5-6 hours on low heat setting or 3 hours on high. Remove bay leaf from pot. Slice or shred beef and place on hard rolls. Skim fat from broth. Pour broth into individual serving dishes, about ¼ cup per person. Before each bite, dip sandwich into broth, then eat.

## Serves 10-12

# Main Dishes/ Meats

# Savory Lamb Kabobs

The Mountain States are one of the largest producers of sheep.

> 1 pound boneless lamb sirloin steak,
>    cut into cubes
> ¾ cup grape juice
> 2 tablespoons oil
> 2 tablespoons lemon juice
> ½ teaspoon dried rosemary
> 2 green peppers, cut into 1-inch thick
>    strips
> 2 onions, cut into 1-inch thick slices

Children can measure the grape juice, oil, lemon juice, and rosemary for the marinade early in the day, or make it the day before. Place the lamb in a bowl or plastic bag and pour the marinade over the meat. Refrigerate until ready to cook.

Drain marinade. Place lamb on skewers alternating with pepper and onion. Grill for 10-15 minutes, brushing with marinate, until lamb is cooked to desired doneness. (Discard marinade.)

An alternate method is to place marinated lamb in broiler pan and broil in conventional oven, close to heating element for about 7-8 minutes for each side.

Serve over a bed of rice.

Serves 4

# Black Bean and Rice Casserole

Beans are a staple of cowboys and others who live or travel the Mountain States.

3 cups cooked brown rice
1 cup cooked black beans, drained
1 (4-oz.) can chopped mild green chili
    peppers
1 large onion, chopped
1 clove garlic, minced
4-oz. (1 cup) shredded Monterey Jack
cheese
1 (8-oz.) carton cottage cheese or
    farmer's cheese
½ cup grated Cheddar cheese

Preheat oven to 350°F. Grease a 2-quart casserole dish.

Children can help measure and mix rice, beans, chilies, onion, and garlic in a large bowl. Pour ⅓ of the mixture into the prepared casserole dish. Sprinkle with half the Monterey Jack cheese and half the cottage cheese. Repeat layers, ending with rice mixture.

Bake for 20 minutes. Sprinkle with Cheddar cheese. Bake 10 minutes longer, or until cheese is melted and slightly browned.

## Serves 6-8

# Smothered Hash Browns and Ham

Ham makes this a hearty main dish.

4 baking potatoes
2 tablespoons oil
1 onion, chopped
1 green pepper, diced
1 cup diced ham
1 cup Cheddar cheese
Salt and pepper, to taste

The day before: children can help scrub potatoes under cold water. Just before baking, prick with a fork 3 or 4 times to allow steam to escape. Bake for 1 hour, or until soft. Cool, refrigerate overnight.

An adult can heat oil in a large skillet over medium heat. Add onion and pepper and sauté until lightly browned. Meanwhile, grate the unpeeled potatoes with a hand grater. The potato skin will not go through the grater; discard the skin.

Remove the onion and pepper from the skillet and set aside. Add grated potatoes to skillet and fry until browned, turn and let crisp a few more minutes. Add onion, pepper, ham, and cheese to skillet and heat a few minutes, just until cheese is melted. Children can season with salt and pepper; serve immediately.

Serves 4

# Vegetables/Side Dishes

# Baked Potato Bar

The Mountain States, especially Idaho and Colorado, are big potato producers. Potatoes grow under the ground. To harvest them, they need to be dug up. That is why potatoes look dirty and are sometimes caked with dirt. Did you know there are basically two kinds of potatoes, one for baking and one for boiling? They are easy to tell apart because they are two different colors: the light skinned is for baking and the red skinned is for boiling.

> **4 medium to large baking potatoes**
> **Salt and pepper to taste**

Preheat oven to 400°F.

Children can help scrub potatoes under cold water. Prick with a fork 3 or 4 times to allow steam to escape. Bake for 1 hour in conventional oven or about 12 minutes (3 minutes per potato) in microwave until soft.

Meanwhile, prepare toppings. When the potatoes are cooked, serve immediately. Pass the bowls of toppings at the table, family style, so each person takes the amount they desire.

## Toppings:

Can use butter, sour cream, chives, cooked and diced ham, chopped hard boiled eggs, sautéed mushrooms, chopped cooked broccoli, and others.

Serves 4

# Campfire Potatoes

5 red potatoes, peeled and thinly sliced
1 medium onion, sliced
6 tablespoons butter or margarine
1/3 cup grated Cheddar cheese
2 tablespoons minced fresh parsley
    or 2 teaspoons dried parsley
1 tablespoon Worcestershire sauce
Salt and pepper, to taste
1/3 cup chicken broth

Children can help place potato and onion slices on a large piece of heavy-duty tin foil (about 20-by-20-inches). Dot with butter or margarine. Sprinkle with cheese, parsley, Worcestershire sauce, and salt and pepper. Bring up foil-edges into a bowl-like shape and add broth. Fold foil up, bringing edges together. Seal by turning edges down and crimping. Place on grill, covered, over medium heat for 35 to 40 minutes or until potatoes are tender.

*Serves 4–6*

# Confetti Corn
Corn is another popular, hearty food of the Mountain States.

3 slices bacon
1 onion, chopped
1 green pepper, diced
1/4 pound fresh mushrooms, sliced
1 (15-oz.) can whole kernel corn, drained
1 (15-oz.) can chopped tomatoes, with juice
1/2 teaspoon sugar
Salt and pepper, to taste

Fry bacon until crisp in a large skillet over medium heat. Remove and set aside. Add onion and pepper to skillet; fry until lightly browned, about 5 minutes. Add mushrooms. Fry 2 minutes longer. Add corn, tomatoes, and sugar. Bring to a boil. Season with salt and pepper. Pour into a serving dish. Children can crumble bacon and put on top.

*Serves 4–6*

# Spinach with Balsamic Vinegar

1 tablespoon butter or margarine
1 pound fresh spinach
¼ cup balsamic vinegar

Rinse spinach. Children can help remove stems by pinching them off. Discard stems. Pour vinegar into a small pitcher and place on the table. An adult can melt butter or margarine in a large skillet over medium-high heat. Add spinach leaves and cook 1 minute or just until spinach wilts. Serve immediately with vinegar.

*Makes 4–6 servings*

# Desserts

## Easy Fruit Cobbler

1 stick butter
3 cups berries or other fresh fruit such
    as apples, pared, cored and sliced
¼ cup sugar
2 teaspoons lemon juice
1 cup flour
½ cup white sugar
½ cup brown sugar
1 ½ teaspoons baking powder
¼ teaspoon salt
1 cup milk

Preheat oven to 400°F. While oven is heating, melt butter in a 9-inch square pan.

Prepare fruit and mix with ¼ cup sugar and lemon juice; set aside.

Children can help measure and mix flour, sugars, baking powder, salt and milk in a medium-sized bowl. An adult can pour the batter over melted butter in pan; do not stir. Spoon fruit mixture over top of batter. Bake for about 45 minutes or until browned. Best served warm with vanilla ice cream.

Serves 6 - 9

# Snacks

## Shelly's "No-Bake" Snack Bars

*Hot mixture is poured over the cereal/fruit mixture to make these breakfast bars.*

2 ½ cups crisp rice breakfast cereal
½ cup oatmeal (quick cooking)
½ cup coconut
¾ cup wheat germ
2 cups granola
½ cup corn syrup
½ cup white sugar
2 tablespoons molasses
½ cup peanut butter
½ teaspoon vanilla
½ cup raisins

Grease a 9-by-13-by-2-inch pan.

Children can help measure and mix crisp rice, oatmeal, coconut, wheat germ, and granola in a large bowl; set aside.

Children can help measure corn syrup, white sugar, and molasses into a small saucepan. An adult can heat this mixture to boiling over high heat, stirring with a wooden spoon until sugar melts. Remove from heat and add peanut butter and vanilla.

Adult is to pour this mixture over cereal mixture as this is very hot. Add raisins and stir well.

Pour into prepared pan. After they cool slightly, use a buttered piece of waxed paper to press evenly in pan. Cool completely and cut into squares.

*Makes 24 servings*

# Pacific Coast Region

**Alaska**
**California**
**Oregon**
**Washington**

## Activities:

- Pretend you are traveling on the Oregon Trail in a covered wagon. Describe foods that might be available along the trail. What food would you take with you?

- Make a "sewing card" outlining the trip west. Glue a map of the United States to cardboard. Mark the Oregon Trail. Punch holes every inch or so. Use yarn and a big, blunt needle to sew the trail. Display on the fridge.

- Make a caramel apple dip: melt together ½ cup apple juice, 7 oz. caramels, unwrapped, 1 tsp. vanilla, ½ tsp. ground cinnamon, ⅓ cup creamy peanut butter. Serve with apple wedges.

- Go fishin'. Make a fishing pole out of a stick or dowel. Attach a magnet to the end of a string. Tie the string to the stick. Cut out fish shapes from construction paper. These can be simple or elaborate: simple figure-eight fish or made to look like real ones. Use your imagination. Attach a paper clip to each fish and scatter them over your "ocean floor." Now go catch the big ones.

- Pretend to ice fish. In order to fish when the water is frozen, Alaskans cut a hole in the ice and drop their fishing poles down into the water. To pretend you are fishing, turn a cardboard box upside down. Cut a hole in the box. Cover the box with foil or blue construction paper. Create paper fish, see activity above, "Go Fishin'." Put the fish in the hole. Drop the magnet in to catch the fish.

• Conduct a snow experiment. Collect clean snow in three cups. Place one bowl in the freezer, one in the refrigerator, and one on the counter. Check to see how long each takes to melt.

## Regional Description

The rugged coast of the Pacific Ocean forms the western border of this region. Mountains with their snow covered peaks are visible to the east. This coastal zone, often called the Pacific Northwest, reaches from northern California to southern Alaska.

The region's climate is influenced by the surrounding mountains. Precipitation is high along the coast, but short distances away it is more arid. Because of its fertile area and rainfall, the Pacific Coast States produce more vegetables and fruits than any other region of the United States.

Hundreds of different crops are grown here. This area is a top producer of more than 45 fruits, vegetables and nuts. It is also a large producer of milk, eggs, sheep, and enjoys the abundance of fish and seafood. California leads the nation in kiwi, sweet cherries, lemons, melon, peaches, strawberries, asparagus, avocados, broccoli, carrots, cauliflower, lettuce, bell peppers, tomatoes, almonds, and walnuts. Washington leads in apple production. Oregon is one of the top producers of potatoes, pears, and hazelnuts.

Most of Alaska is too cold, too mountainous, or too dark to grow many fruits and vegetables. Because Alaska has a large coastline, fish and seafood are their major businesses. Salmon, shrimp, halibut, and herring are plentiful. Restaurants boast of Alaska King Crab legs.

# Appetizers

## Salmon Spread

Fish is one of the foods in abundance along the Pacific coast.

> 1 (15-oz.) can salmon, or 1 pound fresh, cooked salmon
> 1 (8-oz.) package cream cheese, softened
> ½ small onion, chopped fine
> 1 tablespoon lemon juice
> ½ teaspoon horseradish
> Salt to taste
> Chives (optional)

Adult can open can of salmon. Let cream cheese soften at room temperature for an hour before starting, or place in microwave for 1 minute on defrost or low. Chop onion.

Children can mix together salmon, cream cheese, onion, lemon juice, and horseradish. Both adults and children can taste mixture, add a sprinkling of salt, get a clean fork and taste again. Chill 2 hours or overnight. Serve on crackers or as a dip for celery. Sprinkle with chives, if desired, to add color and flavor.

*Makes about 2 cups*

# Salmon Canapés

The texture and taste of salmon when it is smoked is totally different than when it is fresh. Smoked salmon, also called "lox," is wonderful on sandwiches, especially when combined with cream cheese.

1 (8-oz.) container (whipped) cream cheese
1 loaf, appetizer size, pumpernickel bread, sliced
¼ pound sliced smoked salmon
Cherry tomatoes, cut in slices
Capers

Children can help spread cream cheese on bread. Top with a slice of salmon, a slice of tomato, and a caper. Serve immediately or refrigerate until ready to serve.

*Serves about 6 as an appetizer*

# Breads

San Francisco is noted for their Sourdough Breads. See recipe on page 201.

# Oven-Baked Apple Pancake

The state of Washington grows more apples than any other state. Serve this for breakfast, a light lunch, or dessert.

2 tablespoons butter or margarine
1 cooking apple, such as Granny Smith
½ cup whole wheat pancake mix
⅓ cup milk
2 eggs, beaten
¼ cup sugar, divided
2 tablespoons chopped nuts
¾ teaspoon cinnamon

Preheat oven to 450°F. Melt butter or margarine in a 9-inch glass pie plate in the oven. Pare, core, and slice apple. Place apple slices on top of butter or margarine. Bake for 5-7 minutes to soften. Meanwhile, mix up batter. Children can help measure pancake mix, milk, eggs, and 1 teaspoon of the sugar into a medium-sized bowl. Stir to combine. Batter will be lumpy.

Scatter chopped nuts on top of apple slices. Pour batter on top of nuts and apples. In a small bowl, children can mix remaining sugar and cinnamon. Sprinkle on top of batter. Cover with foil. Bake for 10 minutes. Remove foil and bake for an additional 3-5 minutes, until lightly browned. Serve in wedges.

Serves 2-4

# Soups, Salads, and Sandwiches

# Cheesy California Mix Vegetable Soup

*This savory soup is sure to become one of your family's favorites!*

4 cups chicken broth or 4 cups water plus
    4 bouillon cubes
1 quart mixture of fresh broccoli,
    cauliflower, and carrots or 1 (16-oz.)
    bag California Mix frozen vegetables
2 medium-sized red potatoes, pared and
    diced
2 cups water
2 tablespoons cornstarch
1 pound processed cheese

Heat broth or water and bouillon to boiling in a large (4-quart) pot. If using fresh vegetables, rinse broccoli and cauliflower. Trim and cut into bite-sized pieces. Pare carrots, rinse and slice. Add to the broth along with potatoes. Bring back to boil, turn down heat and simmer for about 10 minutes, or until tender.

If using frozen California Mix vegetables, add now, and simmer an additional 5 minutes until vegetables are tender.

Stir together water and cornstarch. Add to pot while stirring. Cut cheese into large cubes, add to pot and stir until cheese has melted. Serve immediately.

*Serves 4–6*

# Bow Tie Pasta and Chicken Salad

Fresh vegetables are key to Pacific coast cooking. This recipe combines fresh vegetables, chicken, and pasta for a light yet satisfying meal.

1 (8-oz.) package bow tie pasta, cooked
    and drained
1-2 chicken breasts, cooked and diced
1 tomato, diced
1 cucumber, pared and diced
1 cup chopped fresh broccoli
1 (8-oz.) bottle Ranch dressing
Mixed greens
Avocado

Children can help mix all ingredients except greens and avacado in a large bowl. Chill for an hour or more. Serve on a bed of mixed greens with avocado slices on the side.

Serves 4

# Laura's Apple Salad

3 eating apples, such as Gala, Delicious or Jonathan
1 cup halved grapes
1 cup sliced celery
1 cup miniature marshmallows
½ cup chopped walnuts (optional)
1 cup mayonnaise or salad dressing
¼ cup sugar
½ tablespoon lemon juice

Adult can core and dice apples, leaving peel on. Children can help measure and mix apples, grapes, celery, marshmallows, and nuts in a large mixing bowl. In a small bowl, stir together mayonnaise, sugar, and lemon juice; pour over apple mixture and toss. Best if mixed 20-30 minutes before serving; chill before serving.

**Note: If you need to prepare this salad early in the day, soak apple pieces for 5 minutes in orange juice or lemon-lime soda to prevent browning.**

Serves 8

# Tempting Sandwich Suggestions:

The Pacific coast offers some wonderful sandwich combinations using the characteristic fresh vegetables and fruits, combined with meat, poultry or fish on a variety of breads.

- Breast of turkey, avocado, crisp bacon, Cheddar cheese on multigrain bread
- Sautéed portabello mushroom, lettuce, tomato, mayonnaise on croissant roll
- Walnuts, avocado, alfalfa sprouts, lettuce, mayonnaise on French roll
- Tuna salad with alfalfa sprouts and almond slices on oatmeal bread
- Avocado, Monterey Jack cheese, tomatoes, alfalfa sprouts, spinach leaves, mayonnaise on pumpernickel bread
- Chicken salad with almonds and apples on sourdough bread
- Grilled chicken breast, bacon, Swiss cheese, tomato and lettuce on onion roll
- Tuna topped with melted Cheddar cheese on whole wheat bread
- Hot roast beef, American cheese on grilled potato bread
- Turkey breast, asparagus spears, and melted Cheddar on Kaiser roll

# Tuna Patties

2 (7.5-oz) cans tuna
¼ cup finely chopped onion
¼ cup finely chopped green pepper
½ cup mayonnaise
1 tablespoon lemon juice
½ cup bread crumbs
2 eggs, beaten
½ teaspoon salt
2 tablespoons oil

Children can stir together tuna, onion, green pepper, mayonnaise, lemon juice, bread crumbs, eggs, and salt.

Adult can heat oil in a large skillet over medium heat. Using a large spoon, drop tuna mixture into skillet to form 4 to 6 patties. Sauté about 5 minutes on each side, or until brown. Serve on a bun with mayonnaise and sweet pickles.

*Serves 4*

# Wild Game Burgers

*Can substitute ground beef or ground turkey for the wild game.*

1 pound ground wild game meat, such as
    deer meat
1 teaspoon salt
1 ½ teaspoons horseradish
2 teaspoons prepared mustard
1 ½ teaspoons Worcestershire sauce
3 tablespoons ketchup
¼ cup chopped onion
½ cup soft bread crumbs  OR 1/ 4 cup
    dry bread crumbs
¼ cup evaporated milk or light cream
4 hamburger buns

Children can help measure and mix all ingredients. Form 4 patties. Wash hands.

Adult can broil patties close to broiler coil for about 6-8 minutes on each side, depending on the thickness of the burger. Remove from heat. Children can sprinkle with salt and pepper. Serve on toasted buns with favorite burger toppings.

*Serves 4*

# Main Dishes / Meats

# Walnut Chicken Stir-Fry

The Pacific Coast Region states are top producers of nuts, such as almonds, hazelnuts, pistachios, and walnuts. This chicken dish gets its distinctive flavor and crunch from the walnuts.

2 teaspoons cornstarch, divided
3 tablespoons soy sauce, divided
1 pound boneless, skinless chicken
    breasts, cut crosswise into strips
1 tablespoon water
1 ½ teaspoons vinegar
1 ½ teaspoons sugar
½ cup walnut pieces
3 tablespoons oil
1 green pepper, cut into strips
½ teaspoon ginger

Children can help measure ingredients. Measure 1 teaspoon cornstarch and 1 tablespoon of soy sauce into a medium-sized bowl; add chicken and stir to coat. Set aside. Meanwhile, combine remaining teaspoon cornstarch, remaining 2 tablespoons soy sauce, water, vinegar, and sugar in a small bowl; set aside.

Heat oil in a large skillet or wok over medium-high heat. Add walnuts and sauté a few minutes, or until toasted. Use a slotted spoon to remove walnuts from the pan, and set aside. Add green pepper to skillet, cook and stir about 3 minutes; remove from skillet.

Add chicken to skillet and stir-fry about 5 minutes or until cooked through. Add ginger. Stir vinegar mixture and add to skillet heating a minute or two, until bubbly and thick. Return green pepper to skillet; top with walnuts and serve over rice.

Serves 4

# Best Salmon Bake

1 (16-oz.) salmon fillet
¼ cup mayonnaise
Salt & pepper to taste
1 onion, sliced
1 lemon
½ cup chicken broth or bouillon

Preheat oven to 350°F.

Place salmon fillet in a greased casserole dish, skin side down. Children can sprinkle salmon lightly with salt and pepper and spread on mayonnaise, using a butter knife or spatula. Top with onion slices. Adult can cut lemon in half and remove seeds with a fork. Squeeze fresh lemon over all. Pour broth around salmon. Cover and bake 20 minutes or until salmon flakes. Serve with *Cucumber Sauce;* see next page.

# Cucumber Sauce

1 small red onion
1 cucumber
Salt
½ cup sour cream
¼ mayonnaise
3 tablespoons finely minced fresh dill

Adult can peel and slice onion and pare cucumber. Children can seed and slice cucumber and sprinkle both sides of the vegetables with salt; set aside. After 30 minutes, place the vegetables in a colander and rinse with cold water. Drain well and dry them on a dishtowel.

Adult can dice cucumber and onion and place in a medium-sized mixing bowl. Children can measure and mix in the sour cream, mayonnaise, and dill. Refrigerate a few hours before serving to blend flavors. Serve with hot or cold fish dishes. This is especially good with salmon.

Serves about 6

# Vegetables / Side Dishes

# Red Cabbage Slaw

1 head red cabbage, shredded
1 red onion, sliced thinly
1 green pepper, sliced thinly
¼ cup sugar
Juice from 1 lemon
Juice from 1 orange
1 teaspoon salt
½ teaspoon celery seed
1 teaspoon dry mustard powder
½ cup oil

Begin the day before. Children can help layer cabbage, onion, and pepper in a large bowl (a glass bowl shows the pretty colors). Children can help measure sugar, lemon juice, orange juice, salt, celery seed, dry mustard powder, and oil in a medium-sized bowl. Use a wire whisk to combine ingredients.

Pour over layered vegetables, but do not mix. Cover and refrigerate overnight. Just before serving, toss until well mixed.

Serves 8

# Asparagus with Cheese Sauce

1 pound fresh asparagus
½ teaspoon salt
2 tablespoons butter or margarine
2 tablespoons flour
1 cup milk
1 cup grated Cheddar cheese
¼ teaspoon dry mustard

Rinse asparagus, using a vegetable scrubber, if needed. Cut off the ends where the stalk is tough and discard. In a large skillet, heat about ½-inch water and salt to boiling over high heat; add asparagus spears. Turn down heat to low, cover and simmer 8-10 minutes, until spears are tender, but not mushy. Drain. While asparagus is cooking, make sauce.

Children can help measure butter, flour, and milk. An adult can melt butter in a small, 1-quart saucepan over medium heat. Add flour and stir. Add milk and stir constantly until mixture boils. Turn down heat to low; stir in dry mustard and cheese. Serve over asparagus.

Serves 4

# Green Beans with Almonds

1 (10-oz.) package frozen French cut
    green beans
1 tablespoon butter or margarine
2 tablespoons slivered almonds

Children can help prepare green beans. Cook green beans according to package directions. Drain.

Meanwhile, an adult can melt butter or margarine in a small skillet over medium heat. Add almonds. Sauté for just a few minutes, until lightly browned. Add green beans and toss, just to mix. Serve immediately.

Serves 4

# Orange Couscous

Naval oranges have a "naval" or "button" on one end. They are best for eating, rather than for juice. Some naval oranges are called California (eating) oranges and others are called Florida (juice) oranges.

½ cup orange juice
½ cup water
½ cup chopped green pepper
1 teaspoon butter
⅛ teaspoon salt
⅔ cup couscous (a type of pasta)
1 naval orange, peeled, cut into bite-size
    pieces
3 tablespoons chopped green onion

Children can help measure orange juice, water, pepper, butter, and salt in a medium saucepan. An adult can place on range, over high heat. Bring to boil; remove from heat. Stir in couscous; cover. Let stand 5 minutes. Stir in orange and green onion.

*Serves 4*

# Fruit Relish

In the Alaskan wilderness, people hunt for game such as elk, moose or deer. Serve this fruit relish with roast game, chicken, or pork.

**1 cup diced rhubarb**
**½ cup cranberries or blueberries**
**½ to 1 cup sugar**

Children can help measure fruit into a bowl. An adult can grind the fruit using a grinder or food processor. Add sugar to taste. Chill until ready to serve. Serve in a pretty dish.

*Makes 1 ½ cups*

# Desserts

# Applesauce Mix-in-the-Pan Cake

This is a quick and easy recipe with a pleasing taste and texture.

1 ⅔ cups flour
1 cup packed brown sugar
1 teaspoon baking soda
1 ½ teaspoons allspice
½ teaspoon salt
½ cup applesauce
½ cup water
⅓ cup oil
1 teaspoon vinegar
Powdered sugar

Preheat oven to 350°F. An 8-by-8-inch pan is your "mixing bowl." Children can help measure flour, brown sugar, baking soda, allspice, and salt into pan. Stir with a fork. Mash any lumps of brown sugar. Add applesauce, water, oil, and vinegar. Stir with a fork until combined. Use a rubber spatula to get into the corners.

Bake for 35 to 40 minutes, or until wooden tooth pick comes out clean. For a pretty topping, children can shake a strainer with a spoonful of powdered sugar over cake. No need to frost.

## Variation:

Chocolate Chip Chocolate Cake: Omit allspice and applesauce. Add ¼ cup cocoa to flour mixture. Increase water to 1 cup. Add ½ teaspoon vanilla when adding water. Sprinkle ½ cup semisweet chocolate chips on top of batter before baking.

Serves 9

The Pacific Coast Region is the number one producer of over a dozen varieties of fruits. Strawberries are one of the most popular crops. Grapes are one of the most valuable crops.

# Grape Freeze

You can use any amount of grapes. Children can rinse grapes, pat dry and pull off vine. Adult can cut in half. Place on cookie sheet. Place in freezer. After a few hours, or the next day, use as "ice cubes" in drinks, or spear with a fork and nibble on for a frosty snack.

**Caution: prevent young children from choking by cutting the grapes in half before freezing.**

# Easiest Strawberry Dessert

**1 pint fresh strawberries**
**1 cup powdered sugar**

Children can help rinse strawberries. (Leave them whole with stem intact.) Place sugar in a pretty bowl, in the center of a plate, surrounded by strawberries. Serve. To eat: dip strawberry into sugar and eat.

# Chocolate Dipped Strawberries

> 1 (6-oz.) package semisweet chocolate chips or chocolate candy-making disks
> 1 pint fresh strawberries

Place chocolate chips in a microwave safe dish or in a double boiler on the range. Melt on low power or over low heat to prevent burning. Meanwhile, children can help rinse strawberries. Dry *completely*. Leave strawberries whole with the stem intact.

Pour melted chocolate into a bowl. Children can help dip strawberries by grasping stem and dipping half of strawberry in melted chocolate, so that part of the pretty red color of the fruit is still showing. Place on a cookie sheet lined with wax paper. Refrigerate to help chocolate set and to keep strawberries fresh. Store covered in refrigerator. Eat within two days.

# Strawberry Cream Dessert

> 2 (3-oz.) boxes strawberry gelatin
> 1 pint fresh strawberries or 1 (10-oz.) package frozen strawberries
> 1 cup (½ pint) whipping cream

Children can help to prepare gelatin as directed on box. Use a large glass bowl, or 9x13 pan. If using fresh strawberries, rinse, stem and cut in half. Add fresh strawberries to cooled gelatin mixture. (Frozen strawberries can be added to hot gelatin mixture.) Place in refrigerator until almost set.

Point out how the cream looks before it's beaten. Adult can whip cream with electric beaters until soft peaks form or children can use a rotary beater. Observe how the cream has changed. Children can fold whipped cream into strawberry mixture. Place back in refrigerator until set.

## Serves 8-10

# Peppermint Mints
*Peppermint oil is one of the products of the Pacific Coast States*

> 1 (3 oz.) package cream cheese
> ½ teaspoon peppermint extract
> 2 drops green food coloring
> 2 ½ cups sifted powdered sugar

Take cream cheese out of refrigerator to soften about an hour before starting, or place in microwave for 1 minute on defrost. An adult can blend cream cheese, peppermint extract, and food coloring with an electric mixer. Gradually add powdered sugar to cream cheese mixture. If the mixture gets too stiff, continue with a wooden spoon.

Knead the mixture in the bowl using the heel of your hands in a pressing, folding, turning motion, until smooth. Add additional sugar, if needed to keep the dough from sticking. Children can help roll dough into small balls, place on wax paper and flatten with a glass. Or, if you have rubber candy molds, dip ball in powdered sugar before pressing into mold. Pop out shape and place on wax paper lined cookie sheet. Refrigerate overnight.

## Makes about 48 mints

# Hawaii

## Activities:

- Create a centerpiece. Children can place kiwi, apricots, strawberries, navel oranges, and avocados in a large bowl. Or another centerpiece idea is to place palm fronds or green leaves in a glass bowl with shells.
- Have a Hawaiian Luau. Choose a warm day for your luau, or party. Make leis, or Hawaiian necklaces, by cutting colorful tissue paper into flower shapes and drinking straws into one-inch pieces. String enough of these on dental floss for everyone at your party, or have your guests create their own. Serve punch with a fresh fruit slice on each glass. Wear your bathing suit and grass skirt if you have one. Eat outside or inside on a beach towel.
- Make shell necklaces. Compare the beautiful shapes, coloring and markings on shells. Find one with a hole and string a ribbon through for a necklace. Shells protect the soft bodies of water creatures. Although most shells are found at the seashore, some shellfish live in fresh water or on land.
- Taste different juices. Buy three types of juice. Pour a little into fancy stemware. Taste juice and see which one you like the best. Serve with crackers and cheese.
- Make a melon boat for a party. Buy three types of melons - watermelon, honeydew, and cantaloupe. An adult can cut the melons

in half, lengthwise. Children can use a melon baller to scoop out melon balls. Use watermelon half as a bowl to hold the melon balls.

## Regional Description

Hawaii consists of over 100 islands, but only seven are inhabited, or have people living on them. These islands were formed from volcanic eruptions, which make them very fertile.

Hawaii is considered an island paradise, growing tropical fruits such as bananas, pineapples, guavas, and papayas as well as macadamia nuts, sugarcane, ginger root, and coffee. Hawaii provides many different kinds of fish and seafood.

Like much of the USA, Hawaiian food is a melting pot of cultures. Polynesian, Filipino, Korean, Portuguese, Japanese and Chinese influence is evident in many delicious Hawaiian dishes.

# Beverages

# Hawaiian Punch

The characteristic red punch is popular with people of all ages.

12-oz. frozen orange juice concentrate
or 4 cups fresh orange juice
12-oz. frozen guava juice concentrate
or 4 cups guava juice
12-oz. frozen pineapple juice concentrate
or 4 cups pineapple juice
½ cup red Grenadine
1 cup ginger ale

If using frozen juice concentrate, mix according to package directions.
Children can help measure and mix juices together in a large bowl. Chill.
Add Grenadine and ginger ale just before serving.

*Makes 1 ¹/₂ quarts*

# Quick and Easy Punch

1 (64-oz.) bottle fruit punch
1 (46-oz.) can pineapple juice
1 (2-liter) bottle ginger ale

Chill ingredients the night before. Children can help pour ingredients
into a large punch bowl.

*Makes 6 quarts*

# Appetizers

## Red and White Shrimp Dip

What a pleasing combination of flavors!

1 (8-oz.) block cream cheese
1 (12-oz.) bottle cocktail sauce
1 (6-oz.) can or 6-oz. fresh baby shrimp
Wheat crackers

Children can unwrap and place cream cheese on a dinner plate. Pour cocktail sauce over cheese. Place shrimp on top. Serve with crackers to scoop shrimp, sauce and cheese.

*Makes about 10 servings*

# Breads

# Pineapple Bread

½ cup crushed pineapple
⅔ cup bran cereal
1 egg, beaten
2 tablespoons oil
2 cups flour
¼ teaspoon baking soda
2 teaspoons baking powder
1 teaspoon salt
½ cup sugar
¾ cup chopped macadamia nuts
    or almonds

Preheat oven to 350°F. Children can grease a 9-by-5-by-3-inch loaf pan.

Drain the can of pineapple in a strainer held over a cup measure. Add water to make ⅔ cup liquid. Pour liquid over bran cereal; let set 10 minutes. Children can help measure and add: egg, oil, flour, baking soda, baking powder, salt, sugar, and nuts to bran mixture. Stir just until combined.

Bake for 65 to 75 minutes or until toothpick comes out clean when inserted into center of loaf.

*Makes 1 loaf*

# Chocolate Macadamia Muffins

1 ⅓ cups flour
⅔ cup sugar
½ cup cocoa
1 ¼ teaspoons baking powder
¾ teaspoon baking soda
¼ teaspoon salt
⅔ cup semisweet chocolate chips
⅔ cup chopped macadamia nuts
⅔ cup buttermilk
¼ cup oil
1 egg, beaten
½ teaspoon vanilla

Preheat oven to 350°F. Grease or line muffin tin with 12 paper muffin cups.

Children can help mix flour, sugar, cocoa, baking powder, baking soda, salt, chips, and nuts in a large bowl. Make a well in the center. Add buttermilk, oil, egg, and vanilla. Stir just until all ingredients are combined. Fill muffin cups ⅔ full. Bake for 20 minutes or until a toothpick inserted into the center of the muffin comes out clean. Best served warm.

*Makes 12 muffins*

# Salads

## Pineapple Fruit Bowl Salad

Pineapples are common in Hawaiian dishes because of their large pineapple plantations. We are lucky to have these fresh fruits available in the grocery store. One beautiful way to serve a fruit salad is by using a halved pineapple as a bowl or "boat."

1 pineapple
1 banana
1 papaya
1 mango
1 kiwi

Adult can cut pineapple in half lengthwise, leaving the leafy "crown" on one half. Cut and scoop fruit, leaving about a ½-inch rim of fruit around the edge. Discard the woody center. Cut pineapple into chunks and place in a large bowl. Prepare remaining fruit. Children can help peel and cut soft fruits into chunks with a butter knife. Add to bowl and toss. Spoon and heap fruit into pineapple boat. Use as a centerpiece.

### Serves 6–8

# Ambrosia Salad

1 cup pineapple chunks
1 cup mandarin oranges
1 cup flaked coconut
1 cup miniature marshmallows
1 cup sour cream or plain yogurt

Children can help measure and mix all ingredients together in a bowl.
Chill before serving.

Serves 6-8

# Main Dishes/ Meats

# Luau Spareribs

A luau is a party with food and entertainment. These spareribs are the perfect size for little fingers.

1 rack pork spareribs, about 1¾ pounds
¼ cup soy sauce
2 tablespoons honey
2 tablespoons fruit juice
½ teaspoon black pepper

Place the spareribs, meaty side down, in a 9-by-13-by-2-inch glass baking dish. Children can help measure and mix soy sauce, honey, fruit juice, and black pepper. Spoon the sauce over the ribs. Place in the refrigerator overnight. Place ribs, meaty side up, on a roasting pan. Bake ribs in a roasting pan at 350°F. oven for 1½ hours or until done. Discard marinade. Slice into ribs before serving.

Makes 10-14 ribs, or about 4 servings

# Waikiki Meatballs

*Beautiful Waikiki beach is a big tourist spot. A sweet and sour sauce makes these meatballs really delicious!*

1 pound ground beef
1 egg
½ cup fresh bread crumbs
1/4 cup chopped onion
2 tablespoons milk
2 tablespoons soy sauce
¼ teaspoon hot pepper sauce
½ teaspoon salt
⅛ teaspoon garlic salt

## Sauce

⅔ cup sugar
½ cup apple cider vinegar
½ cup pineapple juice
1 ½ tablespoons soy sauce
1 teaspoon salt
1 ½ teaspoons cornstarch
2 tablespoons cold water

Children can help measure and combine: ground beef, egg, bread crumbs, onion, milk, soy sauce, hot pepper sauce, and salt in a large bowl. Roll into small meatballs. Adult can fry meatballs in a skillet over medium heat, turning to brown on all sides. Drain and set aside.

For sauce, children can help mix sugar, vinegar, soy sauce, and salt in a medium saucepan. Adult can heat to boiling over high heat, stirring frequently. Turn down to low and simmer 5 minutes. Mix cornstarch with water in a small bowl. Add to sauce to thicken. Gently stir meatballs into sauce. Serve over rice.

*Serves 4*

# Sweet & Sour Marinade for Tangy Baked Chicken

1 tablespoon sesame seed
½ cup soy sauce
2 tablespoons cider vinegar
1 clove garlic
1 teaspoon minced ginger root or
    ¼ teaspoon dried, ground ginger
1 tablespoon sugar

Children can help measure and mix sesame seed, soy sauce, and vinegar with a wire whisk. Adult can mince garlic and ginger root. Add to soy sauce mixture, along with sugar, stirring to dissolve sugar. Use to marinate chicken in Tangy Chicken Bake (see next recipe), or refrigerate until ready to use.

**Note: ginger root can be found in the produce department of the grocery store. Remove the hard, outer layer with a knife before using.**

*Makes ³/₄ cup*

# Tangy Baked Chicken

1 recipe Sweet & Sour Marinade
1 (4 pound) roasting chicken, cut up

The day before, mix up recipe for marinade. Rinse chicken under cool water. Place chicken in a 3-quart casserole dish or large plastic bag. Pour marinade over chicken. Turn chicken over. Refrigerate overnight.

Preheat oven to 400°F. Turn chicken over. Place chicken in 9-by-13-by-2-inch glass pan. Discard marinade. Bake for one hour, or until cooked through. The skin will become thin and crisp.

Serves 6

# Desserts

# Banana Cake

1 cup white flour
½ cup whole wheat flour
½ cup brown sugar
1 teaspoon baking powder
1 teaspoon cinnamon
⅛ teaspoon salt
2 bananas, mashed (about 1 cup)
¼ cup applesauce
1 egg, beaten
1 teaspoon vanilla

Preheat oven to 350°F. Grease and flour a 9-by-9-inch square pan.

Children can help measure and mix flours, sugar, baking powder, cinnamon and salt in a large bowl. Make a well in the center and add banana, applesauce, egg, and vanilla. Pour into prepared pan.

Bake about 20 minutes or until a toothpick inserted in the center comes out clean. Cool. Sprinkle with powdered sugar or spread with a butter cream frosting. Cut into squares.

*Makes 9 servings*

# Quick and Easy Coconut Pie

1 (3.4-oz.) box instant coconut cream
    pudding mix
1 ¾ cups milk
1 9-inch graham cracker crust

Children can help measure and mix pudding mix and milk, following directions on pudding box. Add coconut, pour into pie shell and chill several hours or overnight before serving.

*Serves 8*

# Coconut Pudding

3 cups frozen coconut milk, thawed,
    Or 2 cups fresh or canned coconut
    milk and 1 cup regular milk, Or
    3 cups regular milk and 1 ½ cups flaked
    coconut
½ cup sugar
½ cup cornstarch
⅛ teaspoon salt
1 teaspoon vanilla

Grease a 9-by-9-inch pan. Children can mix together sugar, cornstarch, and salt, then add to coconut milk in a medium-sized saucepan. An adult can heat on medium, stirring frequently, until thickened. Add vanilla. Pour into prepared pan. Chill for at least 1 hour before serving. Cut into squares. Serve with whipped cream and tropical fruit, such as pineapple, banana, papaya, mango or kiwi, and plain cookies, such as vanilla wafers.

**Note: if using canned milk, shake well before using.**

*Makes 9 or more servings*

# About the Author

Although Amy Houts now lives in the rural northwest Missouri town of Maryville, she was born in New York, and has lived in several states including Maryland, Kansas, Tennessee, and Mississippi. Living in different regions of the USA helped her experience the delicious cultural foods of each area. Writing about them helped her discover the variety and abundance of American food.

*Cooking Around the Country With Kids: USA Regional Recipes and Fun Activities* is the second in her "Food and Fun" series of cookbooks for children. Her first in this series is *Cooking Around the Calendar with Kids: Holiday and Seasonal Food and Fun*, which won the Missouri Writers' Guild Major Work Award. More information about this award winning book can be seen at http://www.ImagesUnlimitedPub.com.

Amy is the author of more than three dozen books for children. Her passion is educating children through her writing. She has written math, science, and social studies subjects as well as concepts for preschool-age children featuring the TV cartoon character Dora the Explorer. Amy instructs over 100 students in a correspondence course on writing for children through the Institute of Children's Literature.

Amy and her husband, Steve, a seventh grade science teacher, have two grown daughters, Emily and Sarah. Amy spends her days mostly at home, writing and teaching, in the company of her adorable boxer-mix, Pepper.

You can contact Amy at amysase@gmail.com.

# Other Books and Publications by Amy Houts

## Books

- Seven picture books from Korean Hemingway, upcoming, 2010.
- A book for adults from David C. Cook, upcoming, 2009.
- *Active Bible Play*, David C. Cook, 2009.
- *Count with Diego Go, Diego, Go! Mini-Activity Book.* Learning Horizons, upcoming, 2009.
- *BOZ the Bear's Big Book of Bible Fun: God's People & Me.* David C. Cook, 2008.
- *Do Animals Talk?* Pearson Learning Group, 2008.
- *What is It?* Pearson Learning Group, 2008.
- *Clap, Clap: Clapping Games.* Pearson Learning Group, 2008.
- *Yoga.* Pearson Learning Group, 2008.
- *Think Like a Scientist.* Pearson Learning Group, 2008.
- *She Digs Rocks.* Pearson Learning Group, 2008.
- *Symmetry Crafts.* Pearson Learning Group, 2007.
- *The 100th Day of School.* Pearson Learning Group, 2007.
- *Make and Use an Abax.* Pearson Learning Group, 2007.
- *Let's Exercise!* Pearson Learning Group, 2007.
- *Pattern Fun.* Pearson Learning Group, 2007.
- *Make an Animal Craft.* Pearson Learning Group, 2007.
- *Sesame Street Countdown with the Count.* Learning Horizons, 2006.
- *Dora the Explorer Preschool Adventure.* Learning Horizons, 2006.
- *Dora the Explorer Addition.* Learning Horizons, 2005.
- *Dora the Explorer Subtraction.* Learning Horizons, 2005.
- *Dora the Explorer Safety.* Learning Horizons, 2004.
- *Dora the Explorer Trace & Draw.* Learning Horizons, 2004.
- *Cooking Around the Calendar with Kids.* Images Unlimited, 2001.
- *Winifred Witch and her Very Own Cat.* Dalmatian Press, 2001.
- *On the Farm.* Dalmatian Press, 2000.
- *The Princess and the Pea.* Dalmatian Press, 1999.
- *Tigers in the Wild*, and Shawn South *Aswad*, Dalmatian Press, 2000.

- *Learning Through Cooking Activities.* Preschool Publications, 1993.
- *An A\*B\*C Christmas.* Standard Publishing, 1993.

## Articles for Adults and Children

Honeymoon for Four," *Cup of Comfort for Divorced Women*, Adams Media, 2008.

"Wind Energy," SCORE! Educational Centers, www.scorelearning.com, 2008.

"Fingerprints," SCORE! Educational Centers, www.scorelearning.com, 2008.

"Not-So-Fast-Food," Focus on the Family Clubhouse, July, 2008.

"Hometown Hero Tom Brand: Cruising for Charity," American Profile, June 11, 2006.

"Creating a First Aid Kit," *American Profile*, December 25, 2005.

"Holiday Gifts from the Kitchen," *American Profile*, November 20, 2005.

Approximately 250 Feature Stories/Reporting, *Nodaway News Leader*, 8/99–8/05.

"Homemade Ice Cream," *American Profile*, July 31, 2005.

"Carving a Jack O' Lantern: a fun, family tradition," *American Profile*, October 17, 2004.

"Easter Eggs," *American Profile*, April 4, 2004.

"Let's Talk Turkey," *American Profile*, November 30, 2003.

"POW Network Helps Find Answers," *VFW Magazine*, September, 2003.

"Cut Food Costs," *American Profile*, October 5, 2003.

"What's for Lunch?"*American Profile*, August 10, 2003.

"Gifts for the Graduate," *American Profile*, April 6, 2003.

"A Valentine Celebration," *Ladybug*, February, 2003.

"Encouraging Hope in Young Children," *My Self, My Family, My Friends: 26 Experts Explore Young Children's Self-Esteem*, Preschool Publications, Inc., 2000.

"Science in the Kitchen," *Ladybug*, November, 2000.

Monthly column, "Preschooler in the Kitchen," in *Parent and preschooler Newsletter*, Preschool Publications, Inc., 1986-1998.

## Stories for Children

"When Daddy Comes Home," *Military Life: A Children's Anthology.* Elva Resa Publishing, upcoming, 2010.

"When Mommy Comes Home," *Military Life: A Children's Anthology.* Elva Resa Publishing, upcoming, 2010.

"Coming to America," 2008, SCORE! Educational Centers, www.score-learning.com, 2008.

"Andrew and the Auction," SCORE! Educational Centers, www.scorelearn-ing.com, 2008.

"Racing to the Principal's Office," SCORE! Educational Centers, www.scorelearning.com, 2008.

"The Lunchroom," SCORE! Educational Centers, www.scorelearning.com, 2008.

"Where?" *Babybug,* November, 2000, reprinted, August, 2008.

## Poetry for Children

"My Mom," *Programs for Children,* Standard Publishing, upcoming 2009.

"My Dad," *Programs for Children,* Standard Publishing, upcoming 2009.

"The Legend of the Christmas Spider," *Christmas Programs for Children,* Standard Publishing, 2007.

"Little Spiders Trick or Treat," *Ladybug,* October, 2006.

"Christmas Wonder," *Christmas Programs for Children,* Standard Publishing, 2003.

"Counting Rhyme, " *Ladybug,* August, 2003.

"Month by Month with Mop," *Ladybug,* January, 2002. Cooking verses for each month with correlating recipes on-line.

"Snowman Smiles," *Holidays and Seasonal Celebrations,* January/February, 2002, reprinted in *The Big All-Year Book of Holidays and Seasonal Celebrations,* 2002.

"Snakes Never Slurp Their Soup: a time for table Manners," *My Self, My Family, My Friends: 26 Experts Explore Young Children's Self-Esteem,* Preschool Publications, Inc., 2000.

"Oh Rats!" *Lollipops,* May/Summer, 1997.

"Christmas Night," *Sunshine Magazine,* December, 1990.

"The Five Senses of Christmas," *Alive! for Young Teens,* December, 1985.

## Plays for Children

"Get Ready! For Baby Jesus," Christmas Programs for Children, Standard Publishing, 2003

"If I had Lived When Jesus Lived," Easter Program Book, Standard Publishing, 1996

## Activity Place Mats

Diego Activity Place Mat: Numbers. Learning Horizons, upcoming 2009

LeapFrog Activity Place Mats: ABC, healthy food, addition, money. Learning Horizons, 2006

## Song Lyrics

"Snakes Never Slurp Their Soup: a time for table manners," Think, Play, Dine (Don't Whine!) kit with CD, Learning Horizons, 2008.

## Awards

She Digs Rocks, Missouri Writers' Guild Best Juvenile Book Award, honorable mention, 2009.

"When Daddy Comes Home," Military Life: A Children's Anthology Finalist. Sponsored by Elva Resa Publishing and MilitaryFamilyBooks.com, 2008.

LeapFrog Activity Place Mats: ABC, healthy food, addition, money. Dr. Toy Best Vacation Children's Product Award, 2006.

Dora the Explorer Subtraction. Missouri Writers' Guild Best Juvenile Book Award, third place, 2006.

Dora the Explorer Safety. Missouri Writers' Guild Best Juvenile Book Award, 2005. Creative Child Magazine "Seal of Excellence" award, 2004.

Cooking Around the Calendar with Kids. Book Sense 76 March/April 2002 pick, Missouri Writers' Guild Major Work Award, first place, 2002.

Winifred Witch and her Very Own Cat. Missouri Writers' Guild Best Juvenile Book Award, second place, 2002.

Missouri Writers' Guild, for prose and poetry, 1990, 1992, 1993, 1997, 2002, 2005, 2006, 2009.

# Recipe Index

# General Index

# Snaptail Books Order Form

Yes, I want to order **books for children, parents, teachers, grandparents. Perfect for homes, libraries, schools, home-schools.** Please send me:

|  |  | Quantity | Total |
|---|---|---|---|

**Cooking Around the Country With Kids: USA Regional Recipes and Fun Activities** an American Heritage cookbook for kids and grown-ups — $19.95 _____ _____

**Cooking Around the Calendar With Kids: Holiday and Seasonal Food and Fun** easy recipes & fun with children
Soft cover $14.95        Hard cover $24.95 _____ _____

**Listening to the Mukies and Their Character Building Adventures** read-aloud stories about relationships — $14.95 _____ _____

**The Littlest Christmas Kitten** children's full color storybook about the night Jesus was born and the kittens' reaction — $16.00 _____ _____

**Our Apple Tree** children 3-10 learn about the life of a tree and the animals that visit. Wonderful for school tours — $6.95 _____ _____

**From the Apple Orchard — Recipes for Apple Lovers** revised and expanded classic apple cookbook — $14.95 _____ _____

**Apples, Apples Everywhere — Favorite Recipes From America's Orchards** apple growers best recipes — $14.95 _____ _____

**Apples** wonderful little book with colored apple pictures, apple history, and apple lore — $17.95 _____ _____

Coming soon…
**Low Sugar, No Sugar Apple Cookbook** — $15.97 _____ _____

Postage: $4.95 for 1 book and $.70 for each additional book _____

Missouri residents add 7.975 % tax _____

TOTAL _____

I understand I may return any of them for a full refund — for any reason, no questions asked.

Name_____

Street_____

City_____State_____Zip_____

Charge to _____Visa _____M/C   Acct. #_____

Exp. Date: _____ Signature_____

Phone Number_____E-mail_____

Or make check or money order payable to Images Unlimited, P.O. Box 305, Maryville, MO  64468

CPSIA information can be obtained
at www.ICGtesting.com
Printed in the USA
FSHW01n0116240518
48424FS